Head to Head

How to run your school effectively

edited by

Vivian Anthony & Robin Pittman

John Catt Educational Limited

Managing Director: Jonathan Evans - Editor: Derek Bingham

Published 1992

by John Catt Educational Ltd.
Great Glemham, Saxmundham, Suffolk IP17 2DH
Tel: 0728 78666

Managing Director: *Jonathan Evans* - Editor: *Derek Bingham*

ISBN: 1 869 863 38 0

Set and designed by
John Catt Educational Limited

Printed and bound in Great Britain by
Bell & Bain Ltd, Glasgow

Foreword

The Rt Hon The Viscount Whitelaw KT, CH, MC

I believe that today's parents take an ever increasing interest in the quality of their children's education. That is surely an encouraging trend, but it provides a formidable challenge to all those concerned with the running of our schools. That is why *Head to Head*, written by those with great experience of their subject, is a valuable and lively publication. Their views, formed by their independent school experience, have relevance for the maintained sector as well.

Parents rightly expect high quality in education for their children especially when they are struggling to meet the rising cost of the fees required. They are investing in their children's future, and they are entitled to value for money. Nor should anyone concerned with schools of all kinds forget for one moment that the quality of education is not confined to the classroom: the challenge must be faced in all the school's activities.

This at the present time demands such particular skills as the management of staff, at a time when in the interests of controlling expenditure, and so the fees, the pupil/staff ratios have to be closely examined and controlled.

This book contains practical help for dealing with all the problems in education and so deserves to be widely read by all concerned.

Contents

Foreword
The Rt Hon The Viscount Whitelaw KT, CH, MC

Introduction

Chapter 1
In the Beginning, *Eric Anderson* 1

Chapter 2
The Head and Teaching Staff, *Robin Wilson* 8

Chapter 3
The Head and Staff Development, *Patrick Tobin* 13

Chapter 4
The Head and the Bursar, *David Smith* 20

Chapter 5
How to be efficient, *Robin Pittman* 24

Chapter 6
The Head and contact with Pupils, *Tony Evans* 28

Chapter 7

The Head and the Parents, *John Rees* 34

Chapter 8

The Head and Former Pupils, *Hugh Monro* 37

Chapter 9

The Head and the Governors, *Roger Griffiths* 40

Chapter 10

Marketing your School, *Graham Able* 46

Chapter 11

The Head and Academic Development, *Vivian Anthony* 52

Chapter 12

Developing the Site, *Geoffrey Parker* 59

Chapter 13

The Boarding School Head, *Richard Rhodes* 65

Chapter 14

The Management of Change, *Michael Mavor* 71

Chapter 15

And finally . . . the School's Philosophy, *Rev Dominic Milroy, OSB*........... 76

Introduction

'Headmasters have powers at their disposal with which Prime Ministers have never yet been invested'. So wrote Churchill in 1930. That authority may now be somewhat tempered – or at least more subtly exercised – and Heads are no longer the autocratic figures of yesteryear. However a person assuming a headship for the first time finds himself or herself in a new vocation very different from the deputy's or departmental post vacated only weeks before.

Various managerial and training courses are now available for the novice Head and serve an invaluable purpose. This book attempts to complement and supplement what may be gained from them.

Fifteen current or recent Heads, all members of The Headmasters' Conference, here attempt to pass on practical advice over the wide spectrum of tasks and responsibilities that face both new and established incumbents. It is guidance garnered from the agony and ecstasy of many years' experience.

The contributors have necessarily drawn on their knowledge of secondary schools in the independent sector, but their reflections and counsel have relevance for those taking up headships, and indeed for Governors, in all parts of a very fluid educational scene in which the demands of management are ever increasing and where the need for wise and informed leadership has never been greater.

Vivian Anthony
Robin Pittman

Chapter 1

In the Beginning

Eric Anderson

Head Master, Eton College

Dear John,

Many congratulations. Lanchester is a good school and you will make it even better. The Governors have found a round peg for a round hole and I feel sure you'll enjoy the challenge as much as the school will enjoy having Alison and you in the Headmaster's house.

When it was announced that I was coming here, Peter Pilkington told me that the six months between appointment and arrival would be my most enjoyable as Head Master of Eton – flattering attention on all hands and no responsibilities whatsoever! He had a point, although fortunately I have enjoyed actually doing the job even more. The six months before you arrive are important though as well as pleasurable and, at the risk of stating the obvious, I'll pass on such crumbs of wisdom as I have now gleaned.

The first rule is not to haunt your new school. You've got a job to finish where you are, and your predecessor has a job to finish and farewells to enjoy. He may feel he should invite you to Speech Day, the School Concert, Sports Day, the School Play, and so on, but don't go. If you do, all eyes will be on you, rather than him, which is not fair on him and not good news for you. Your main advantages in September are that you are new and unpredictable. Don't throw these away by appearing in walking-on parts the previous term.

I would advise you and Alison to go to Lanchester only twice. There ought to be one occasion planned round you, probably a party for the whole staff so that they can all say that they've met you and that you "seem very nice". You will need a separate session with your predecessor to get the horse's mouth account of what you need to know about your new colleagues, the problems facing the school and the decisions which are pending. If he can be persuaded to let you have his diary, or a photocopy of it, for the whole of his final year that will give you a useful insight into the greater and lesser occasions for which you will have to prepare.

If I were you, I shouldn't waste his time by asking him about routines, discipline, timetable or finance. It's better to learn about these when you move in during the summer holidays. The Second Master, Director of Studies and Bursar will speak very freely then and your sessions with them before the term starts are the ideal way to begin to build your relationships with these vital allies.

You may be asked to help with staff appointments, but I'd avoid that if you can. Of course you will want to be involved if it's a very senior or personal appointment, like Second Master, the Head of your prep school or the Headmaster's secretary. But you are actually badly placed to make

Eric Anderson: ". . . information cascades in on you. The painter wall-papering our dining room at Abingdon told us where three of the previous year's leavers had been trying (unsuccessfully) to grow cannabis".

judgements because, however good you are at summing people up, you simply don't have a feel yet for what is right for Lanchester. So if you can, try to persuade the Second Master or the prep school Head to stay on an extra year. For ordinary teaching appointments I'd be inclined to steer clear.

In other words, I believe in brief handovers. That way you give no hostages to fortune and no promises you may live to regret – and you still have the gloss of novelty when you arrive. An admiral once told me that the new captain of a battleship spends only half-an-hour with his predecessor. You'll need a little longer than that, but don't overdo it. The school magazine will want to interview you before you arrive and possibly the local paper. Say "Yes" to both of those, but be careful. Both will ask what plans you have for Lanchester, and your new colleagues will submit what you say to microscopic textual analysis. Newspapers are not places for policy announcements. By all means talk about your past; don't miss the chance to say what has already impressed you about Lanchester, but limit your stated ambitions for the future to getting to know the school and the town as quickly as possible and to continuing the excellent progress made under your predecessor. In fact you don't yet know what needs to be done, but keep quiet about that: you'll know within one term !

How will you know? Well, information cascades in on you. The painter wall-papering our dining room at Abingdon told us where three of the previous year's leavers had been trying (unsuccessfully) to grow cannabis. A day-boy at Shrewsbury, unaware that his new Headmaster was at the next table in Sidoli's Coffee House, gave an aunt a spellbinding account of midnight escapades. Wives gossiping to Alison by the school pool, shop-keepers welcoming you both to the town, local Governors dropping in to see you are settling in, maintenance men putting the house to rights, the Bursar and Second Master in lengthy discussions with you, next term's Head of School who comes to spend a day with you, colleagues who take pity on the family still living out of packing cases and ask you in to meals - all these, intentionally and unintentionally, feed you information and views which you are going to find useful. They will teach you a lesson, too: that there is usually more than one side to each story and you'd better not be too hasty in making decisions.

The summer holidays before you begin are a kind of limbo. You are not quite Headmaster yet, and people feel they have a licence to speak more freely than they will do once everything that goes on is your concern and everything that goes wrong is your fault.

You may learn something too from local people, even if it is only the melancholy and universal truth that neighbours always believe that the school's pupils are untidier and less well behaved than they used to be. What will surprise you is how quickly you are considered a local figure. At Abingdon we slipped into a side pew at St Helen's Church on our first Sunday, only to be welcomed from the pulpit during the announcements. Total strangers, who have seen your photograph in the local paper, give you a nod of welcome in the streets and you quickly realize that even on a family outing you are no longer a private person. Former Headmasters say that one of the delights of retirement is being able to go shopping in old clothes again.

It's a great help in dealing with the local community to have subscribed to the local paper for the six months before arrival. You'll come across a surprising number of the people mentioned in it during your first weeks in the school.

Is the Headmaster's house in a reasonable state after your predecessor's 15-year reign? I guess it will need some renovation. My advice is that you get that done right away. I wish we had insisted on that at Eton. It's tempting to think that it's better to get settled in first and then decide what has to be done, but in a year's time you'll know everything else that needs to be done in the school and feel guilty about spending money on yourself. Don't be greedy, but do insist that they do what ought to be done right away. If it does mean a chaotic month or two domestically, that is a price worth paying, for it's no bad thing if people feel sorry for you at the start!

The school ought to furnish your study for you, but you'll need to stamp something of your own personality on it from the start. A captain of industry once told me that at the very least a new manager should place his desk in a different place from his predecessor's. That decision can say a lot about your style of management. Are you going to face people across a desk as they come in to see you, place yourself so that you can swing to join the circle of chairs round the fireplace, or what? And how are people to reach you? Is your door to stand open (in America, since Watergate, no one seems to shut office doors any more); will people simply knock and come in, or will they first make an appointment with your secretary? You'll need to work that out before the first day of term.

The Director of Studies and the Head of Department in your own subject will want to know how much you are going to teach. Most of us rather fancy ourselves as teachers and are tempted to accept

Eton College: "However good the 'management team', schools remain hierarchical places and an awful lot comes to you for decision or action".

the offer of an A level set. But beware! You'll be too busy to prepare or do your correction properly and you'll be horrified how often you have to ask colleagues to cover for you because you have entry interviews, or a prep school prize-giving or a visiting dignitary or a Governors' meeting to cope with. They'll cover of course but they'll grumble, and your pupils too may grouse to their friends that they are getting short-changed as the exam draws near.

The most helpful bit of practical advice I had as a young Headmaster came from Roger Young. He suggested that a Headmaster should be timetabled for no teaching but instead, at the beginning of each week, should look through the diary and offer to relieve colleagues of a period or two. They are pleased to have unexpected free periods and their pupils are quite flattered to have a visit from the Headmaster. You won't do them any lasting damage in a period or two (in fact, it's easy to be wonderfully stimulating when they aren't going to see you day after day) and you'll get a fair idea of the capabilities of pupils at every level in the school. You may not want to do that every year, but it's good advice for your first year.

If the school has an appraisal scheme, I'd suggest you suspend that for your first term in favour of seeing everyone individually for half-an-hour. You can start by inviting each Head of Department before the end of the holidays to discuss A level results with you: that naturally leads to talk about who has taught well or less well and what the department's problems and ambitions are. During the term ask everyone else to come to see you in turn to tell you what they do in the school, how the school could help them to do it better, what personal and professional hopes they have for the future. You'll learn more about them that way than in half a dozen casual meetings; you'll acquire over the term a good sense of what makes the school tick, and you'll come away with some very good ideas. You'll also acquire an enviable reputation for being a good listener.

What you don't realize until you start is how busy you are going to be. When I was an assistant master I remember dropping in on the Headmaster occasionally to share with him my latest bright idea. He always seemed to have time for me and I occasionally wondered how he filled his days. I know now, and so will you very soon. There isn't a lot of time for twiddling your thumbs.

However good the 'management team', schools remain hierarchical places and an awful lot comes to you for decision or action. You've heard your present colleagues say "Well, I'll give in on that if the Headmaster tells me I must, but not otherwise" and you can now brace yourself for acting as umpire in that sort of dispute. Pupils rightly feel that you are their final court of appeal. Parents will not necessarily be fobbed off with Form Masters, Tutors or Housemasters: the nice ones occasionally, and the awkward ones always, insist on going to the top. Old Boys need you and only you as speaker at their dinners and consultant at their committee meetings. The local community holds you responsible for the behaviour of your pupils and also feels free to call on you for after-dinner speeches and help on civic occasions.

You are also the school's public relations expert, dealing with applicant parents, keeping in touch with the primary and prep schools which send you boys (which often means preaching or giving away prizes or attending governors' meetings at times that are very busy in your own calendar) and occasionally fielding the local or national press. It's exhilarating keeping all these balls in the air simultaneously, but it's very hard work.

Fortunately, you have an understanding wife who'll enjoy being part of the Lanchester community and will be a real help to you. You'll also need a good secretary. You'll quickly learn that if you're not very careful you'll become the slave of the diary she keeps for you. If you don't mark in your daughter's Speech Day at the very start of the term, Alison will be going on her own because you've committed yourself to seeing applicant parents that afternoon. If you don't block off the occasional afternoon for just walking round games you'll find three weeks have gone by when you haven't had a chance to see what's going on.

Somehow (although I've never worked out how) you have to leave time for crises. These generally arrive at the most awkward moments. I felt sorry for the retiring Headmaster I once saw pulled away from lunch on his final Speech Day by a Housemaster who had discovered drugs in his house, but I recognized the timing as typical. However, I hope you're lucky enough to have one really nasty crisis to deal with in your first month. Whether it's drugs or mass drunkenness, systematic bullying or a master eloping with a colleague's wife, there's no better way of earning your spurs. New colleagues feel sorry for a man dealing with a crisis that is not of his making, and they'll be impressed and relieved if you deal with it coolly and fairly.

Actually you will have to begin earning your spurs during the first week of term. It's an extraordinary hurdle race – your first beginning-of-year party for the staff, first Housemasters' meeting, first masters' meeting, first school assembly, first talk to new parents, and perhaps even your first sermon on the Sunday. You really mustn't trip on any of those hurdles. Everyone is watching you and everyone is judging you. It's some consolation that actually they're all hoping you'll do well. It matters terribly to the teachers that the new boss is a success. It matters to the Governors that they are seen to have made the right decision. It matters to parents that their offspring are going to be in good hands. The only people who are not much worried about your performance are the pupils. They are still at the age when change may mean change for the better, and if you turn out to be even worse in their eyes than the last Headmaster, well that's just an act of God. I still remember summoning the Head of School at Abingdon to tell him in advance of the rest of the school that I was leaving for Shrewsbury. We had got on very well and I suppose I expected some expression of regret. "Oh," was his response, "the Governors will have to find another one then." A useful reminder that Headmasters are not as indispensable as they come to believe.

Personally I don't go for great policy pronouncements, or 'mission statements' as they're called today. I'd rather have a feeling of business as usual at the first masters' meeting than platitudes and rash promises. Assemblies may be different. You may want to give some indication of the things you look for and the practices up with which you will not put. Ask the advice of the Second Master and the Head of School during the holidays and then make your own decision. My view is that the summer Speech Day is the earliest moment at which you want to be caught pontificating in public. By then you can legitimately say where the School seems to you to stand and can suggest the direction in which it ought to move.

Pontificating is one of the occupational diseases of headmastering, as this letter illustrates only too lengthily. You won't entirely avoid it, but fight it off as long as you can.

Some of your colleague-Headmasters, growing old and grey and tired, will grumble that headmastering is not what it used to be. Maybe not, but it's still a wonderful job. You'll be fully stretched; you won't ever be bored; you'll have intelligent colleagues and a wider circle of interesting acquaintances outside the school than you ever dreamed of; you'll have one of the few jobs where your wife can be involved; you'll have the exhilaration of managing a demanding job well, and the satisfaction of feeling that ultimately it is all worth while. There isn't a better job anywhere. Enjoy it!

Yours sincerely,

Eric

Chapter 2

The Head and Teaching Staff

Robin Wilson

Headmaster, Trinity School, Croydon

Regardless of how thoroughly you may have prepared yourself for headship, the reality will be different. As a new Head said last year in *The Times*, when he took his first Assembly sitting alone on the centre of the stage looking down on nearly 1,000 pupils and staff: "It does bring home to you what has happened, that you really are a Headmaster. I had not expected to feel the pressure and the atmosphere."

I remember on my appointment one Governor saying that the job would be fascinating but that I would never again have a relaxed night's sleep. I suppose that's true, not because I am worried by being chucked out as some of our colleagues seem to be nowadays, but because of the ever-changing fascination and challenge of the job and the inescapable responsibility. Remember *Henry IV*? "Uneasy lies the head that wears a crown". It's true.

The question of priorities can be answered simply. Your relationship with your staff is far and away the most critical factor. First impressions are most important. You may have a well-developed strategy for meeting a new class and establishing limits and expectations. Much the same will apply when you meet your new staff. Whatever you do, do not try to copy the manner of your predecessor, or criticize him overtly or covertly. I am sure that you have been working hard on the staff photograph and have pondered what your predecessor chose to tell you. I hope that you were not told too much, as you ought to make your own judgements.

What are you going to be called? Headmaster? Head (ugh)? Sir? Mr Patten? Hugh? How are you going to get to know them? How are you going to let your criteria for staff excellence be known? I remember the day we moved in here. The movers had hardly left when the bell rang. A member of the staff offered us a bottle of claret, and thought we might like to join his little wine club. Within a week I had met all the staff but one. When I found him, he said that he knew I would be very busy learning the staff so felt he would hold back. I soon learnt that both of these very different types were in the alpha class as teachers. I recall them to illustrate the need to recognise and accept different temperaments and contributions to the corporate work of the staff.

You will soon learn who you can work with, who is reluctant to change, who is deliberately opposed to all you propose, who is excellent, who is misplaced and what the cliques and hierarchies are. Before long you will have to devise a strategy to shape the staff to work in a way which suits your vision. It all takes time and patience, but you should have a chance before long to influence the composition of the staff. It is normal that a new Head, particularly after a long reign, acts as a catalyst for staff movement.

What sort of Head do you intend to be? The days of the Olympians are over. I don't mean those stern-looking, jaw-jutting men in gown and mortar-board whose portraits look down in disapproving amazement at their puny successors. Within recent memory it was possible for a Head to remove staff of whom he disapproved without difficulty. I remember one Head of Department going in puzzlement to his Headmaster after seeing a job advertised in his department, to be told that it was his own and that his services would not be required the following year. Another managed to remove over half his staff within two years. Thankfully we cannot act like this now, but your style is going to determine your school.

One reason I enjoy watching 'One Man and His Dog' is that I recognise an ex-colleague's style: stand still, blow your whistle firmly and expect the staff to follow instructions faithfully and herd the pupils accordingly. (On a bad day his behaviour was closer to Napoleon's in *Animal Farm*.) For a few this will work up to a point. But for most it leads to behaviour reminiscent of a medieval despot, only talking to a few cronies who never challenge a decision or idea, and ultimately leading to the fate of all despots. I hope that you will see yourself as an enabler, a leader and orchestrator striving for that magic formula which makes a corporate effort greater than the sum of its parts. However it is as well to recognise that there is an element of potential despotism in the job and you would do well to remember King Lear's ultimate recognition of the need for a Fool to tell him home truths. Who is your Fool going to be? How can you know what is going on without being intrusive? How are you going to get the best out of your staff individually and collectively?

The Head of an independent school has absolute responsibility for the appointment of staff and indeed for their development within the school. Even though in maintained schools the responsibility lies with the Governors, they would be foolish to override the Head.

We have to assume that you have some choice. You will of course have an idea of the profile you are after. You may have a vacancy in a staid, even Luddite department, or in one which is a collection of prima donnas. In the first case a teacher in tune with modern practice, in the latter a conservative steady scholar might be your ideal. Naturally you will want them to play a significant role in the general life of the school, but I would advise you not to emphasize this too much. It is surprising what talents and enthusiasms unlikely people develop under the corporate momentum of a good staff.

You will be under pressure to spend a fortune on advertising. You might prefer to take the view that teachers seriously looking for a post will read the normal columns of the *TES*. Let's hope for a good response. You will soon learn to read CVs and references as much for what they don't say as what they do. A lack of clarity about dates, a lack of definition of degree status or A level results, a significant gap – what happened between 1984-6? – a CV may seem clinical, but is in fact very revealing. As for the letter of application, the word processor has a lot to answer for! Letters are becoming too long, too fulsome (how dare he say that he is just what the school is looking for!) and recently too full of NCC/SEAC- speak jargon. Have you heard about the would-be Head who forgot to programme his computer to change the name of the school for which he was applying? I gather he's still trying.

Remember always that you are looking for a human being to teach human beings. This should come through in references (a literary form which needs alert reading between the lines). To take two extremes: if you want to strengthen your English department are you looking for a teacher who can recite all the Statements of Attainment, sub-section by sub-section, or for one who has travelled the world, acted in the Edinburgh fringe, written a play and has then committed himself to teaching? However thoroughly you and your chosen colleagues interview you are ultimately going to have to make a personal judgement. You alone can make it. Do you follow the Head of Department's wish when you know that the department needs the challenge of a different personality within it? If you want an easy life you do, but you would not be serving the school well.

Don't forget to run the necessary checks before the appointment is confirmed, particularly List 99 (of those banned from teaching by reason of relevant convictions). I did once flush out someone through List 99. When I got through to the appropriate department I talked to a very cosy lady who immediately knew the person concerned. "Oh yes, we know him well. He's a naughty lad, is Mr A".

There are many temptations for a Head: to keep the really good staff when you know they are ready for promotion; to accept the mediocre who get by; to hope that the problem staff will quietly go away. You will do well to avoid all these temptations. You have a duty to foster the careers of your colleagues and should indeed welcome movement because a static staff soon stagnates. Remember that excellence for a few years is much more productive than mediocrity for a lifetime, and support your good staff generously in their career ambitions.

More difficult is the development of the mediocre, as they are unlikely to recognise a problem. Persistence and patience from you and Heads of Department can however make remarkable improvements. Younger teachers often take time to find themselves and make serious errors of tactics while doing so. A clear understanding on both sides of the problems, and support while ways are changed, can often rescue a parlous career. On rare occasions you may find yourself in a formal disciplinary case. I am sure you are aware of the care with which the necessary steps have to be taken and logged. The introduction of regular appraisal has been helpful in forcing Heads to think hard about individual members of their staff. Independent Schools are at liberty to devise their own system. I would hope that you will see your personal involvement as being of prime importance for all members of staff.

Suddenly you will no longer be a member of the Common Room, able to relax with your friends and make snide remarks about the Head, the Governors and those colleagues of whom you disapprove. You have inevitably crossed the line. How do you intend to treat the Common Room? Will you wander in whenever you feel like it? Will you regard it as a no-go area where you have no place? I would suggest that neither of these is proper. I find it helpful to be there at morning break when all sorts of little bits of business can be done and you can easily find out what's going on, but not much otherwise. It is very important that staff should have their private space.

Robin Wilson: "Remember always that you are looking for a human being to teach human beings".

As a corporate group are you going to listen to them on all matters, on some or on none? A well-organised Common Room can make an invaluable contribution to developments far removed from their immediate concerns as a social body.

Nowadays we seem to be in continual change, and old patterns cannot cope. It is your job to recognise the need for change, but woe betide you if you simply impose it. Apart from anything else, you will probably get it wrong. Typically, a school will engage every few years in a major curricular review which will affect the pattern of the school day, week or even year. Everyone is affected, and everyone might have something positive to contribute. The orchestration of change is one of your key roles; all too often the timing goes wrong and the project turns sour. My advice would be to adopt the following sequence:

In a 'green paper', float the necessity for change. Make proposals, knowing perfectly well that the ultimate decisions will almost certainly be different. Expect the normal initial defensive reaction; I can predict that the staff will start by resisting a change to the established pattern.

Define a working group which is to consider the proposed changes and, within a strict timetable, invite comments to that group from others. When this working group has met, you will probably be able to monitor the effectiveness of your original proposals, will undoubtedly have gained other proposals and will be able to develop a 'white paper'. One of the best developments of recent years has been the recognition of the need for days devoted to staff and school development. I try to time the discussion of any important issue to tie in with a 'Baker Day'. The white paper will be discussed, involving all staff in appropriate groups, and the results assessed by the original working group.

After all this you, with your closest senior colleagues, have to make the decisions. As the process has meant that all staff feel that they 'own' some of the decisions, you are likely to get the new curriculum or timetable off to a smooth start. Don't forget though that you still have to brief the parents and the Governors clearly.

As I get older I have more sympathy with Polonius. He may have been tiresome – and I dare say there are some on my staff who would like to find me behind the arras – but he gave Laertes much good advice. As the Government exerts tighter and tighter control, as the jargon becomes more and more dominant, hold on to the essential fact that education is about mature human beings teaching developing human beings. You will want around you colleagues of whose attitudes and individuality you approve. You will only deserve to get them, and to keep their support, if you follow Polonius's advice:

> *This above all: to your own self be true,*
> *And it must follow, as the night the day,*
> *Thou canst not then be false to any man.*

Chapter 3

The Head and Staff Development

Patrick Tobin

Principal, Daniel Stewart's and Melville College, Edinburgh

During my exchange year at The King's School, Parramatta, I was handed a slim novel, *The Advancement of Spencer Button*. It is a story to sober the devotees of self-conscious professional development. In the New South Wales teaching service, teachers are posted to schools by the central authority and promoted in pecking order. Young Button is sharp and ambitious. One day he sits down with his wife-to-be, with a list of all the schools in New South Wales, all the present Heads, with dates of likely retirement, and all the teachers who will stand between him and his first headship. Calculation leads to dismay and disillusionment: he will be retired before he achieves the prize. Then a thought hits him. He has not allowed for death, disgrace or dismissal – fates not to be discounted in Sydney – and he revises his estimates, correctly as it transpires. Spencer Button grafts his way to his headship only to find that headship does not necessarily lead to happiness.

It is not the English way of doing things. Here, like A J P Taylor, we believe in the power of accident. Our heroes of literature achieve their headships inadvertently, in schools which they have served all their days and where they have become Mr Chips. Such is the myth. It endures, in reality, in individual teachers who have spent the bulk, or even the whole, of their careers at one school. I read only today in a national paper of a Housemaster who came by accident to Harrow and who has just retired 39 years later. He and his wife committed themselves and their family to their boarding house and worked around the clock for their charges. He also nursed his interest in 17th century French history, wrote textbooks and now has in embryo a further work on Mazarin. For 20 years they have prepared a Herefordshire farmhouse to be their retirement home. Otherwise there was no mention of any professional development, let alone of formal training to meet the requirements of the Children Act, but there can be little doubt that he is a much more fulfilled man than Spencer Button.

We all have our personal experiences. Like the Harrow Housemaster I drifted into teaching – and back to my own school at that – and spent 12 relatively unstretched years in Ealing and Brecon before my appointment to succeed Geoffrey Parker as Head of History at Tonbridge. I had not been there long when one of the Housemasters suggested that I should write to cement the connection which Geoffrey had formed with a particular tutor at Cambridge. The latter replied, disclaiming any acquaintance with Geoffrey Parker but inviting me to visit him. This Cambridge excursion clearly made an impact on Christopher Everitt for, shortly afterwards, when the post of Universities Adviser became vacant, he asked me to take it on. Overnight I became a guru, the purveyor of information and opinion to expectant Housemasters. Rather than disillusion them and discredit myself, I worked very hard, if not always successfully, to mask my ignorance. It was a very English process of professional development.

From Rolls-Royce Tonbridge I moved, via a year on exchange in Parramatta, to Prior Park College, Bath, as its first lay Headmaster. The Christian Brother boarding school, remembered by Peter Levi as an 'artificial paradise running gently to seed', was substantially unchanged 35 years later. My uncomplicated mission was to save it from the dissolution to which the Christian Brothers had originally sentenced it. Before I even arrived I had to appoint one third of the teaching staff. Nothing in my professional formation prepared me for the strains and stresses of the next eight years. It was a time of struggle, experimentation, success, failure, growth and ceaseless change. Almost without exception my professional development in those years consisted of

Patrick Tobin: "The sea in which I now swim for survival is a sea of paper".

my experience of actually tackling the job. I wonder to this day whether I could have been formally prepared for it.

Now that I am in charge of two Merchant Company schools in Edinburgh, with over 2,500 pupils, about 200 teachers and rather more non-teaching staff, my problems have become more obviously administrative. The sea in which I now swim for survival is a sea of paper. When I trained as an assessor for the new National Educational Assessment Centre, an exhaustive and thoroughly professional process which probes the capability of putative Heads in 12 discrete 'competencies', the clinical diagnosis and mentored development offered through the Assessment Centre scheme suggested very powerfully the gaps in my professional formation.

The schools are prosperous and seemingly secure; the world outside seems feverishly fragile and frenetic; the hard-worked teachers are on their guard against change and distraction. What should professional development mean to them – and to me? Should we content ourselves simply with 'polishing up the act'? Or is the moral of my experience that change is in itself an outcome to be sought?

The good independent school makes formidable demands on its teachers and most feel that they have little time left for formal professional development. Nor does this necessarily grieve them, for they tend to be deeply sceptical about such mechanisms as appraisal, award-bearing courses and management training. If there is a regret it is likely to involve a hankering for the lost world of eccentricity when there were 'characters' in the Common Room. Confronted by a curriculum vitae swamped by courses attended and INSET pursued, an independent school Head of Department will probably ask whether the applicant has ever coached a rugby team. As my first Headmaster said to me, "Good teachers are born rather than made."

And yet? The grand solidity of our old buildings can hide the courage and flair of their builders. Arnold of Rugby was forthright in his call for change: "There is nothing so unnatural and so convulsive to society as the strain to keep things fixed when all the world is in continual progress: and the cause of all the evils in the world may be traced to that natural but most deadly error of human indolence, that our business is to preserve and not to improve. . . . It is the ruin and fall alike of individuals, schools and nations".

The more successful a school is, the more it is potentially at risk of decay through paying excessive respect to tradition and conceding too much advantage to the exponents of the status quo. How many once eminent schools have ebbed gently in public esteem, to the benefit of parvenu establishments which have set out consciously to achieve excellence? How many able young teachers have been denied scope for professional development and the expression of their talents in schools where the great questions are settled, if not in history, then behind closed doors? (I am reminded of Cardinal Heenan who, when asked to name the most desirable attribute a priest could have, is reported to have answered "Obedience".) How many new Headmasters have silently cursed the inertia of communities where the need and scope of reform, so clear to the outsider, are hidden from those whose personal careers have become inextricably entwined with the institutions which they have served with such zeal and devotion?

I have no doubt where I stand. The Head should focus on fostering a culture of professional renewal. If the most important element in any school is the quality of its teachers it is the responsibility of the Head to encourage all staff to look after their professional needs. He should be active in identifying opportunities for colleagues and in helping them to realise them. All the time, he will be keeping in mind his own plans and vision for the school, hoping and working to align these with his colleagues' professional development, within the constraints of financial feasibility.

This is of course what good Heads have been doing since schools began. It is implicit in every decision to appoint and to promote teaching staff – and the independent Head is privileged with freedom in this regard. Heads do not need to have formal systems of appraisal before they begin to assess the competence and potential of their teachers.

Nevertheless, at a time when maintained schools have accepted appraisal, independent schools would be foolish to stand aside. Younger teachers will expect to be appraised. Parents and Governors will find it difficult to come to terms with teachers who shy away from formal channels of accountability. The government itself, through the Assisted Place scheme but also through its criteria for school-based initial teacher training, has the means to manoeuvre independent schools into line.

It may well be that appraisal is particularly necessary for independent schools. It is only too easy for the independent school teacher to become rooted to a particular school. Unlike Spencer Button he accepts the odds against his promotion into management. Most people have powerful reasons, in terms of wife's job, children's education, social life or the problems of moving house, for accepting the status quo. The generous fee discounts to staff children given by many independent schools make them peculiarly vulnerable to the phenomenon of the ageing Common Room.

Today's whizz-kid may easily become tomorrow's extinct volcano. Fixed term contracts for promoted posts should be considered. The man who brought genius to his rugby coaching decides that the time has come to hang up his boots. Are there other ways in which he can make a special contribution to the school? Does the shape of the salary scale militate against ambition? The Headmaster might consider a more attractive salary structure, with bars to prevent the 'switched-off' from sharing its benefits. All such management depends on sensitive handling and on close and exact knowledge. It is important for teachers' morale that it should be seen to belong to a coherent programme of professional development, rather than consist of merely opportunistic responses.

Targets and priorities for staff development should be defined through an effective system of appraisal. Independent schools are currently free to fashion their own systems of appraisal in tune with their particular character. In a relatively large school it is practically impossible for the Headmaster to appraise every teacher in any meaningful sense. Effective delegation is essential and 'line-management' is the most obvious structure for such delegation. It is a positive advantage that the Head of Department should be expected to express and develop accountability for all teachers in the department. The challenge for the Head is to keep a finger on many pulses, to glean the appropriate insights and information and to incorporate them into the reports and plans which will be presented to Governors. He may find it necessary, if he normally works through a 'management team', to entrust particular responsibilities for staff development to one of the team or even to create a new post for this purpose.

In a small school the Head has the opportunity, periodically at least, to interview every one of the teaching staff. Yet the burden of appraising more than a dozen staff every two years would be excessive. Delegation to Heads of Department is not desirable, as most departments will have only two or three members. Help might be found through the Deputy Head or a small body of trained appraisers elected or selected from the most respected members of the Common Room.

Either way, the Head remains responsible for ensuring that the processes of appraisal serve useful purposes and do not degenerate into sterile and perfunctory repetitions of bureaucratic routine. Appraisal will be worthwhile if it promotes the expression of appreciation of curricular and extra-curricular achievement, if it helps to identify problems and obstacles to good teaching, if it effects individual and collective improvement, if it establishes realistic and definitive objectives for the immediate future and if it promotes better contact throughout the teaching hierarchy.

In the early days of appraisal it was common in independent schools to stress the purely positive aspects. Its function was to reinforce rather than criticise. A fireside chat revolved around the points which the teacher wished to raise and was utterly different from the clinical evaluation suggested by the term 'appraisal'. Many independent schools indeed chose instead to speak of a 'review'.

This liberal slant now has to confront the more investigative elements in the government's model whereby observation in the classroom, statistical conversions of raw examination results into 'performance indicators' and the compilation of verbal and written comments will ensure that appraisal amounts to a systematic evaluation of performance.

The independent school Head is also becoming daily more vulnerable to odious comparison. More than any of the teaching staff he has to answer to the Governors for any apparent deterioration in the school's place in the local or national league tables. It is the more important that he should personally promote an enlightened approach towards the role of appraisal in his school's staff development policy. Most of his teachers will be of a high standard. If some are inadequate, there should not be a wait of two years for an appraisal interview to combat neglect or incompetence. A Head should share with the Common Room the belief that it is really extraordinarily difficult to quantify the performance of teachers, but they all will also know that it is dishonest to pretend that such measurement does not or should not take place. What is important is that assessment of each teacher's performance should be in the context of a continuum of personal professional development, set against previous appraisal and against the targets for performance and in-service training which were then defined.

Style will matter. Appraisal should encourage openness, including the voicing of critical opinion. It should also help teachers to come to a clearer appreciation of the difficulties facing management. Subtly it can be the means by which teaching staff can be brought to think of themselves in promoted posts.

Daniel Stewarts' & Melville College Pipe Band: "The schools are prosperous and seemingly secure; the world outside seems feverish, fragile and frenetic; the hard-worked teachers are on their guard against change and distraction."

Above all it should be purposeful and forward-looking. It is incumbent on the Head to ensure an adequate follow-up. From the cycle of individual appraisals should emerge the professional development programme of the school. It should be thoroughly costed and presented to Governors for their formal approval. The next appraisal cycle will provide a measure of its cost-effectiveness.

The cost of in-service training is always likely to be considerable. There was a time when most independent schools had no budget at all for staff development. In the mid-1980s the Professional Development Sub-Committee of HMC called on schools to devote 2% of their salary bill to this end, but it is doubtful whether any members approached this target. The curricular revolution has undoubtedly stimulated in-service training within academic departments, but to the exclusion of much else.

Schools will inevitably need to 'buy in' expertise – through courses, seminars and conferences away from school, the formation of cluster groups, visits to school by professional consultants or the purchase of published material – but economy demands that a large proportion of INSET should be school-based. In this respect independent schools have a great advantage in that they emerged from the 1980s unencumbered by statutory limitations on teachers' hours of service. The Head should work hard to persuade Governors that more generous provision of INSET days will be required and that the teaching staff should be compensated with longer holidays for time spent on professional development.

It would be a pity if all professional development had to be justified in terms of the needs of the school, rather than of the teachers as people. Teachers need time to recharge batteries and fill their tanks. Few teachers experience the benefits of an overseas exchange. For my family it has been a permanent enrichment. Experience of the business world, if properly planned and directed, can also bring benefits to school and teacher alike. Even more enlightened would be the adoption of that great Australian institution – paid long-service leave. An imaginative scheme for periodic long-service leave would expressly affirm the philosophy that the welfare and stimulation of the long-serving teacher should take precedence over the more familiar gods of examination results, economy and continuity.

There are examples already of independent schools which have expanded their professional provision into impressive programmes. Millfield School's programme, for instance, includes out-of-school management training for promoted teachers, games coaching awards, academic course development and further degree studies, but also the school-based participation of academic departments, pastoral staff and management in courses on such subjects as Teambuilding, Interviewing, Appraisal, Women in Education, First Aid, Bullying, Smoking, Drug Abuse and PSE.

A feature of the Millfield programme is the school's current collaboration with Bristol Polytechnic on induction procedures for all levels of appointment and on one-day courses in educational management which will be accessible to all staff with the intention of inducting, training and refreshing. These courses are being developed with Bristol Polytechnic and will carry professional awards. Such alliances between independent schools and higher education institutions, in initial teacher training but also for induction and continuing teacher training, are likely to characterise the most effective professional development programmes during the 1990s.

The 1990s will indeed be a highly significant decade in terms of the professionalism of teaching. The move to school-based teacher training will inevitably promote a sharper awareness of the 'competence' required by teachers, especially in those teachers who are selected to act as mentors to students. The proficiency demanded of these mentors will extend far beyond a narrow competence to teach a specific subject and will extend to all those qualities which will constitute the truly professional teacher.

These qualities include an appreciation of the values which underlie the teaching profession, along with the skills and qualifications required for professional competence. It would be disappointing if the 1990s did not see the formation of a General Teaching Council, independent of government and of trade unions, which served to articulate and promote the specifically professional characteristics of teaching.

Finally the 1990s will witness the movement away from local government control of a number, perhaps the bulk, of maintained schools. Hitherto the local education authorities have been powerful engines for professional development in the maintained sector. Grant maintained schools, like independent schools, will have to 'go it alone' in evolving strategies for professional development and in seeking specialist advice and assistance. It is already clear that the 1990s will spawn a professional development industry. Schools and their Heads will need to be discriminating consumers.

When 'selling' his prototype Educational Assessment Centre, Howard Green liked to cite as a seminal work *In Search of Excellence* by Peters and Waterman, and to refer to their findings in subsequent research that the 'good' schools which went on achieving excellence were those where the school and its management were committed to learning. In this process the role of the Head was critically important. He or she should be a 'lifelong learner'. This, I suspect, is a truth which no Spencer Buttons of the 21st century will ever be able to forget.

Chapter 4

The Head and the Bursar

David Smith

Headmaster, Bradford Grammar School

There are numerous metaphors for the relationship between the Head and the Bursar. One of the more attractive is Cavaliers and Roundheads, with its implication that the Head is an essentially romantic, out-going and charming figure with a due respect for hierarchies – particularly those which put him at the top – while the Bursar is much more hard-headed and dour while displaying little respect for anyone. A better working definition perhaps is the difference between the spending departments of government and the Treasury. This definition ignores the fact that the Head is the major earner of the school's income, of course, but it catches the underlying potential friction between the executive who spends the money and his colleague who tries to save it. There is a tension here. How can it be resolved – or at least exploited?

A simple and attractive model is for the Head to be the boss, but it rarely works out like that in practice. Not only do the Bursar's responsibilities put him in a very strong position to prevent this happening, but Governors also tend to be against it. This is because most Governors understand finance better than they do education (and quite rightly so). They can understand the Bursar's problems and arguments more readily. Financial questions are usually more pressing than educational ones and the consequences of getting them wrong are more obvious and immediate. Governors also tend to prefer Roundheads where finance is involved! So it is unlikely that the Bursar's job description will have him or her reporting to the Head. Fortunately for the Head the converse is equally unlikely.

So if a structural or organisational solution is unlikely, how are the roles of Head and Bursar to be exploited in a fruitful and non-confrontational way? It is at this point that we should pause to consider the Bursar's perspective. There is a sense in which the Bursar's job is equally as lonely as the Head's, if not more so. If the Head can show signs of paranoia at Governors' meetings, then how does the Bursar feel when surrounded and assailed by academic staff? Heads have their own priorities which they can easily come to feel the Bursar does not and cannot understand. The Bursar can feel equally frustrated by a Head's economic innocence, if that is what it is. Moreover in dealing with everyone except his own staff, the Bursar is obliged to work through the good offices of the Head. The Head may feel nothing like the same reticence in telling the groundsman or the caterer how to do their job!

The point I am making is that the Bursar needs the Head's understanding and support – and they both need friends. This is a good basis for a working relationship with the added bonus, if they work at it, of personal loyalty and mutual dependence. It is important to add another factor in the balance of self-interest. Because there is a potential division between the Head and the Bursar, if they do not

Bradford Grammar School: "There are numerous metaphors for the relationship between the Head and the Bursar. One of the more attractive is Cavaliers and Roundheads".

resolve it in a dynamic way then someone else will. The Head and the Bursar can stand together or they can fall apart.

If the Bursar needs the Head, then the Head certainly needs the Bursar. After some years as Head of a voluntary aided school, with distinct financial responsibilities and a helpful and willing local authority to fall back on, and many more as Head of an independent School, I sometimes wonder how local management and grant maintained status are going to work unless a Bursar is appointed to take the financial strain. Financial control not only needs accounting skills which play no part in the Head's training (or certainly have not done so up to date), but also daily attention to cash flow and fund management. Even if the Head has the training or natural acumen to master such tasks, how will he or she ever find the time? Financial control is not like clearing an in-tray, which can be the work of an hour in the morning or put off for a week. It demands, or so it seems to me, constant and detailed attention.

So does plant maintenance. I once spent instructive hours walking around the Victorian buildings of a church school with a Very Reverend Chairman of Governors. I am sure the fresh air did me good, although I did not like going up the ladders. The Dean, for such he was, gave every appearance of enjoying it. I suppose that compared with the fabric of a medieval cathedral it was almost light relief for him and I used to point out that if he fell off supernatural agencies were more likely to intervene than in my case. However, it was an expert and time consuming business, and even if a Head can be found who enjoys it, what problems of human relationships or educational planning are being left to fester in the study while he does the rounds of the buildings? That is the Bursar's job.

If I am suggesting that there are areas of school management best left to the Bursar, and I am pretty confident that the Bursar feels the same about the Head's role in dealing with teaching staff, pupils and their parents, I do not conclude that neither should know anything of the other's work. Quite the reverse. I learned a lot from my outings with the Dean which stood me in good stead when it came to planning major building extensions. When a school expands its plant it is doing so for educational reasons. The buildings house a curriculum or planned extra-curricular activities. They may also house boarders, although there seem to be fewer of them these days than there used to be. Whatever the use, it is educational. The Head must therefore be the chief planner, because his expertise and his vision is fundamental to the project. If he knows what is good for him he will stalk the site during construction as well. It would be foolish to do so without the Bursar at his side however, because once a contract has been signed and the first breeze block laid, then all the Bursar's skills become essential. It is also true, once again, that if the Head and the Bursar walk together then no one can get between them or say one thing to one of them and something else to the other. It follows clearly that the Bursar will need and want to understand the educational thinking which underlies the work he has put in hand.

Planning buildings is therefore an excellent example of the partnership between Head and Bursar which I recommend. It also affords conclusive proof of the leading role which the Head must play in areas of management which some might suggest belong to the Bursar alone. Another prime example is financial budgeting. Drucker, one of the gurus of management theory, has laid it down that 'budgeting is commonly conceived as a financial process. But only the notation is financial; the decisions are entrepreneurial'. Now if the Head of an independent school in the 1990s, or for that matter the Head of a locally managed or grant maintained school, is not an entrepreneur he is nothing. What is more, entrepreneurism is a Cavalier's job! The budget is the school's business plan and for that reason it must be the Head's business.

Once again however budgeting calls for a working partnership with the Bursar, as a study of the elements in the budget will prove. There are two elements – fixed costs and variable costs and, of the two, fixed costs will massively predominate, including as they do salaries and wages, educational resources, occupation and administration costs. The total of these items will certainly exceed 90% of expenditure and it is a fortunate and well run school which has 5% left for development year on year. The Bursar can easily employ that 5% if the Head cannot! It is the 5% or thereabouts which affords the Head's window of opportunity to develop a new course or employ a new teacher or add to the school's resources. I am not talking about major projects which require exceptional funding. If it comes to an appeal, then the Head will be left in no doubt about his position as the school's major earner and Cavalier qualities will be at a premium. But the Roundhead has to balance the books. The need for compromise, mutual instruction and mutual understanding becomes crystal clear. Remember also that this year's opportunity cost is next year's fixed cost. Never be left out of the budgeting process!

On the other side of the balance sheet the fees have to be fixed. It is hard to believe that the Head would willingly be left out of this discussion but it has been known to happen. Heads will not be left out for long if numbers on roll begin to fall. It is self-evidently in the Head's interest to be in the process from the start. Indeed setting the fee level is probably the supreme entrepreneurial decision. It is too important to leave to the Bursar or anyone else. Conversely of course the Bursar will not want to leave it to the Head. Once again the need for co-operation is self-evident.

Most of these remarks assume an environment of growth and educational expansion. In the 1990s however, and perhaps for some years now, many independent schools have had to contemplate a much less buoyant economy. Management of change has been high on the agenda of training courses, but with growth as the underlying assumption. A lot of new Heads will find themselves managing recession in all its facets. Needless to say this goes against the grain of any professional educator. There is no reason to think that Bursars enjoy it either, but planning for contraction or even, in an extreme case, for survival may be a requirement of the times. In such circumstances priorities become crucial and only the Head can judge what must be preserved at all costs. Only the Bursar will know the cost of preserving it. If the two do not try to think as one then a problem can easily become a disaster. This is the final example and a grim one of both my arguments. A Head should be left out of little which concerns the Bursar; but he must always aim to work in step with him and seldom move without the Bursar by his side.

All this is to describe an idealised relationship. For the reason I gave earlier it is unlikely to be hierarchical. However self-interest and idealism combine to dictate that it must be a partnership. If it can be a friendship, so much the better for both. If it becomes a rivalry based upon jealousy or mutual distrust, then both self-interest and good principles combine again to indicate that inefficiency, unhappiness and imminent catastrophe can be the result. There are enough reasons for a Head to be frustrated and unhappy without turning the Bursar into yet another one. At the very least both must observe certain ground rules. They should never seek to score off each other at Governors', staff or parents' meetings or even, I would say, in private conversations with any of these categories. There should be no private agendas. Meetings between the Head and the Bursar should be frequent and regular, even if not continuous. They should take care to explain their areas of work to each other and to justify their individual aims. You see how rapidly we move from rules of combat to the terms of an alliance. An alliance is what this relationship should be and, if it works, then it will be one of the strongest power blocs in the school. At a personal level it can also contribute to considerable serenity!

Chapter 5

How to be efficient

Robin Pittman

Head Master, St Peter's School, York

A reviewer wrote recently that Archbishop Runcie was 'a radical conservative with a self-effacing charisma'. This is perhaps not a bad description of quite a lot of us Heads. For the few whose principles are made of sterner stuff and whose charisma is more public the need to be efficient is probably not so imperative; for us lesser mortals I suspect that good office organisation and some administrative slickness are important elements in our success at running schools.

All of us Heads have our strengths and weaknesses: we are better at some aspects of the job and less good at others. If I am not too bad at organising myself and am fairly business-like at my desk then my efficiency probably serves two purposes: it undoubtedly answers an inner personal need (I have never enquired about my potty training!) and it does give me some elbow room which is useful for one who is not a workaholic and who does not relish toiling in the early morning, late at night or in the middle of holidays.

Also I had early experience (denied to anyone born after 1939) of commanding a desk: I served in the Royal Artillery during my National Service and was fortunate in being made Assistant Adjutant of my regiment for the last nine months of my time. Hence at the age of 19 and 20 I was dealing with piles of paper moving from in-tray to out-tray, taking action on them as appropriate, drafting letters, dealing with secretaries (except that they were called clerks and were male), using the phone and generally being near the centre of a busy administrative operation. This early office baptism gave me a taste for these sorts of tasks and prepared me for the deskwork which is a constant and threatening part of a Head's life and routine. Efficiency here frees one to meet all the many other headmasterly demands that come one's way.

The new Head inherits a secretary and will have the easier life if she is good at all the usual secretarial skills (including being able to write some of the letters) and is quick, discreet and personable. I have been very fortunate in the three secretaries I have had during my two headships, all of them good but in different ways. It is an oft-quoted cliché that being a Headmaster is a very lonely job (it is not as bad as all that and you get paid more) and it is useful if one's secretary can share a confidence, allows one to indulge an indiscretion (so long as she keeps quiet about it) and enjoys a mutual chuckle over some of the absurdities and crises which come one's way.

If however she is an old battleaxe totally wedded to one's predecessor's ways and unwilling to adapt, then the best course is to ease her out and bring in a secretary of one's own choice. But beware of precipitate action: the new Head will face the inevitable staff reappraisal after the honeymoon terms are over. A long-serving secretary being forcibly removed could become the focus of staff criticism

Robin Pittman: "Different Heads doubtless have different ways of keeping in touch".

directed against one. Don't do nothing if she's no good, but go just a little bit gently in the process of replacing her.

Let us assume that the secretarial back-up is first-class and consider how to achieve office efficiency. I strongly suggest the use of a dictating machine; the secretary should throw away her shorthand pad and hone up on her audio-typing. As a young assistant master I remember my own Head being inaccessible between 9 and 10 in the morning while he was closeted with his secretary for dictation in shorthand. This imposed a restriction on him and wasted her time. The dictating machine is a great liberator allowing one to write letters whenever necessary and giving the secretary greater flexibility in arranging her own working routine.

It may be useful if I map out what is for me a fairly typical day so far as administration is concerned. This is not a blueprint for all Heads but it works for me and may contain guidelines helpful to others. I get into the study at 8.00 am. There is then a very valuable 40 minutes before Chapel when I go through the mail, am available for pupils to sign the Merit Book, have a daily chat with the Head of School and am approached by staff desperate to catch me (by 'phone or head round the door).

Concerning the mail, I do what secretaries instinctively don't like: I pick out and open envelopes that look interesting and which may require my attention. Secretaries are wary of this practice because it is important for them to know what is in the post. Letters should not be pocketed; they must be 'processed' with the secretary knowing their contents. By 8.40 despite the interruptions I will have vetted the 15 to 20 letters of the day addressed to me, sent some of them into the out-tray to be dealt with by others, put some aside for later consideration and discussion and answered some on the tape ready for typing up later. Thus before Chapel I will have already dealt with the bulk of the post and looked in the diary to check on the day's structure. I do think that this early start is valuable: it means that from the beginning of the day you and not events are in control – and this creates a better frame of mind (unless there has been a tricky letter in the post) for the spiritual uplift in Chapel from 8.40 to 9.00 am.

As soon as Chapel is over and I am back in the study I have coffee brought in and buzz my secretary. We then have a session lasting not more than 10-15 minutes when I have queries, problems, reminders and tasks for her and she has similar business for me. We go over the engagements for the day (with a look too at the week ahead) and I pass across the opened mail and my tapes. Thus we have both established the day's agenda in a fairly brisk manner before 9.15 am. After that the day seems to unfold with an inevitable momentum of its own dictated by the diary: completing and taping more correspondence, meeting prospective parents, talking to staff, answering the 'phone, interviewing job applicants, drafting speeches, seeing pupils, dealing with crises, even teaching. (By the way a new Head should not take on too heavy a teaching timetable: the Governors have appointed him not to take the fourth year bottom maths set but to be a manager with a very wide range of responsibilities. He should be seen in the classroom; possibly he should do some lessons with new pupils; but he should guard against getting bogged down and clogged up with marking and preparation. He has other priorities.)

Later on in the day one will want to sign letters and seize any opportunity to deal with further external and internal correspondence – and not start the next day clearing up the previous day's backlog. This flow of mail, notes and memos never stops. Leave the office for a meeting or to watch a rugger match and it will have built up in your absence, although a good secretary will be able to keep it in check and deal with some of it on her own initiative. Don't let it all pile up – keep that hour-and-a-half from 5.30 pm for a bath and a read of the evening paper before the dinner party or concert or meeting which will undoubtedly be your lot for three or four evenings a week. There is also a marketing spin-off in keeping the desk fairly clear and tidy: I doubt whether prospective parents are much impressed by a Head whose study is a disordered riot of letters, files, exercise books, cricket bats and anonymous cardboard boxes. I suspect that the state of a Head's desk is as revealing about him and his personality as is the choice of books on his shelves and pictures on his walls.

'Communication' in all its forms is one of the most crucial aspects of headmastering, and while face-to-face and regular communication with certain key people will not guarantee effectiveness it will enhance one's influence and bolster respect for one's leadership. Communication and consult-ation are essential elements too in actually arriving at the right policy decisions (and sometimes the right decision will be the unpopular option). Different Heads doubtless have different ways of keeping in touch. My own technique is to have regular slots when I see particular key people. This ensures contact even when there may not be much currently to discuss. I keep in my desk files for Bursar, Second Master, Chaplain and others, and their contents then constitute the agendas for these unofficial meetings. As I have said already I have a regular early morning chat with the Head of School. Twice a week I have a session with my Second Master-cum-Director of Studies. Once a week I sit down with the Bursar, although we are often popping in to see each other on other occasions. This is always a busy 90 minutes with much to discuss and decide on. I also have weekly slots for the Chaplain and for my Junior School Headmaster. The Chairman of the Common Room and the Sanatorium Sister I see on a monthly basis. I should have a regular session with the School Doctor but the occasional lunch together is a more pleasant if less adequate substitute. This little system does ensure contact on a continuing basis with those who matter particularly and I find it of mutual importance in exchanging information and opinions and in aiding the development of ideas and decision-making. Of course there will also be the regular cycle of Housemaster and staff meetings – equally important but perhaps beyond the scope of this particular homily.

In a slightly different category are my fairly frequent contacts with the Chairman and Vice-Chairman of Governors. It is very relevant to efficiency as a Head to seek an informal chat with the Chairman prior to a Full Board and, in my case here at St Peter's, a similar session with my Vice-Chairman before the meetings of the General Purposes and Finance Committee over which he presides. It is absolutely vital to go through the agenda beforehand in this way: it is an important means of developing positive working relationships between Head and Chairman and Head and Vice-Chairman, and this mutual confidence is essential if and when one encounters rough water. When I started as a Head in 1978 nobody told me how crucial this partnership is, and I only realised the need for it after having gone through a fairly dire crisis involving myself, staff and Governors in my second year (the painful details are still etched on my memory). That was my low point as a Head. Good, informal, regular, frank and confidential links with my various Chairmen subsequently have been a huge bonus and comfort whenever the sea has been a bit choppy.

My last tip is hardly as significant but nonetheless as practical: I have only one diary and carry it home each night and to school in the morning. If there are two diaries, one for school and one for social engagements, then the most awkward muddles develop with one's wife accepting a supper invitation for both when her husband should actually be attending a parents' meeting in the school.

As I said earlier this is 'my way' and, as I am approaching retirement seemingly somewhat faster than Frank Sinatra, new Heads will surely develop their own ways, very probably superior to mine, of keeping efficient and businesslike. However a few hints at the start may be useful for the novice Head in keeping afloat as he develops into a stronger swimmer.

Chapter 6

The Head and contact with Pupils

Tony Evans

Headmaster, The Portsmouth Grammar School

It is an intriguing fact that over a period of years two styles of headship may have disappeared: first, that of the Head who, standing aloft and aloof on the bridge, barked orders to all on the lower deck, whether pupils, staff or parents; second, by strange simultaneity, that of the Head who held open court and received at almost any hour pupils, staff and parents with seeming disregard for strict appointments and on whom time appeared to exert no pressure.

Today's Head works within greater constraints and, in the face of the multifarious pressures exerted upon him or her, it can be all too easy to lose contact with pupils. Yet the welfare of pupils is the rationale of any school. Their happiness and achievement must be the driving ambition of its Headteacher and of all its staff. It is remarkably easy to lose sight of this truth. Pastoral care, in a society of disintegrating values, is the ultimate barometer of a school, on which all other academic and extra-curricular benefits are founded. It is the Head who must set the tone in this and in the matter of values, perhaps more than in any other sphere.

What are the constraints exerted now which can preoccupy the Head to the exclusion of pupils' more personal concerns? Any who has held the position over recent years would speak eloquently of the commercial and managerial pressures now imposed. There has been much talk of a need for Heads to be better managers and indeed for Heads to be recruited from areas of life outside the strictly scholastic. In some cases a Headteacher can be appointed without prior experience of a school and without, one therefore assumes, a primary vocation for leading the young. There are further demands made by building and budgetary considerations and a Head must be concerned with the development of the curriculum (not all of which should be delegated). There are the pressures of public relations, of the increasingly mountainous deliveries of questionnaires, surveys and reports and of the human and diplomatic niceties involved in relationships with staff, parents and Governors and in relations with the locality. Any one of these dimensions to a Head's life can be made the preoccupation of a given day and any one of these can lead to the relegation of contact with pupils. That day can so easily become a week, and the week a term. . .

The Head has always been a more isolated figure in a school community than most. This does not necessarily mean that he or she has to be lonely but there is both an inevitability and a wisdom about the distance between the Head and others in a school. When it comes to adolescents' perception of a Head, it would be unsurprising if he or she were not generally identified with a range of unwelcome concepts and outmoded ideas and something close to adult ignorance of reality. It is not easy for a Headteacher to bridge such a conceptual chasm, born mostly from age and the suspicion of the young for authority and its motives. Nor indeed should a Head in his contact with pupils erode that sense of distance. If a Head becomes too close to pupils, much of the value of his position may be eroded too. Such is the dilemma. Yet by various means he must be perceived as approachable.

Contact with pupils will be on a different scale according to the size and nature of a school community. A Head probably has greater opportunity to know each individual pupil in a small rural boarding school for example than in a large urban day school where hours of work will be more condensed and the catchment area wide. Yet parents will expect of the Head, whatever the size of school, an impossibly detailed knowledge of each pupil and it is a tribute to the enduring interest in the young which characterizes so many Headteachers that knowledge of their pupils is the quality with which most Heads would most wish to be identified. How, in the maelstrom of the working day and week, particularly in the potentially impersonal day school, can such knowledge be acquired?

In a large school community even physical identification of so many pupils can pose an immediate problem for many Heads; yet all pupils would expect to be recognised by him. However artificial the approach to this task may be, it needs to be undertaken. One simple technique to help the Head know his charges is to have group photographs taken of the first year pupils and Sixth Form entrants seated in alphabetical order and to have first name and surname written on the prints under each boy or girl. This is an established Services strategy for learning the names of a new intake and a little regular homework on the photographs can work wonders in increasing the Head's ability to recognise pupils.

Whatever steps a Head takes to know the pupils, there must be an honest acceptance that he will know only a very few very well, a rather larger number quite well, many more by sight and by name and some regrettably not at all. It does not, of course, mean that concern and values cannot be conveyed by the Head in more direct public ways and, as much as seeking knowledge of the individual pupils, a Head must make strenuous efforts to remain apprised of what motivates, worries, excites and disconcerts each age group. The heart and mind must in this sense remain young when the hairline indicates the contrary.

Some would dispute the need for a Head to teach but I would argue that the greatest risk is *not* to teach. It does not much matter at which level the Head teaches or, indeed, how many periods in the week are so occupied. But it does seem, if one is not to lose sight of the vocation for which most of us entered the profession and if pupils are not to perceive the Head as a remote and detached administrator, that personal contact with pupils in this way is critical. Some find it useful to teach their specialist subject, either to the youngest or to those in the Sixth Form. Probably a mixture of both is a good idea and many Heads, particularly in day schools, find it useful to teach perhaps one period a week to new pupils in their first term or year. Others may choose to teach non-specialist work, in General Studies perhaps, or by means of Current Affairs or Religious Studies. The latter is particularly valuable at a senior level: private anxieties or the concerns of the age are quickly discernible for, whereas pupils may choose like staff to hide behind the barriers of technical

Tony Evans: "The Head has always been a more isolated figure in a school community than most".

knowledge in, say, their Economics, French or Physics, there should be few barriers in discussion between the Head and pupils when political and ethical issues are confidently and openly raised.

There can surely be little of such personal value to a Head as teaching and thereby demonstrating to pupils that this remains a central conviction in the Head's life. There can be nothing which affords such direct and regular contact, such confidence and such exchange of views. All else, for the Head rather than for the Housemaster, seems secondary and more superficial. So, too, in teaching the Head can convey a genuine love of a subject and there will be in that very exercise a value conveyed to the pupils as a whole, a message which is transmitted beyond those who immediately benefit (although at the time they may not view things in quite that way).

But on the assumption that a Head will teach, at least for a small proportion of the week, where else might a Head establish with pupils contact of a formative and informative kind? The most obvious means, at least for a knowledge of pupils, is through the school's extra-curricular activities. Whether it is on the touchline or at concerts or plays, by attending quizzes or debates, there will always be an opportunity to establish some sort of social contact. It may only be a few words but those words in themselves can lead to deeper conversations if required. And contact with pupils means knowledge of pupils, of their interests and their strengths. How else can a Head assess reports, redress the balance and encourage?

There are other methods, too, of a rather more formal kind, which can be valuable. Many Heads find it helpful to interview each of the pupils submitting UCCA and other application forms. It is particularly useful at the end of a pupil's career, when a large number of inhibitions can be cast aside, for the Headteacher to spend some time with each, asking the normal questions about the future but also asking more specifically about the past and each pupil's experience of the school, with its strengths and weaknesses, the pupil's regrets and satisfactions. Such an interview, while it may seem remarkably belated, can help the Head later in his contact with younger pupils, in his understanding of the pupil's perception of the school as a community, of its system, its purpose and its shortcomings. Such interviews are invaluable in gleaning from leavers a greater sense of reality than might otherwise be evident and in seeing the school through pupils' eyes. Age, position and our blinkered perception may otherwise prevent such an understanding.

On a weekly basis, with pupils throughout the school, a formal but guaranteed method of contact is what one might term a Distinction system or, perhaps more sensitively, Recognition. If staff are encouraged to send to the Head a pupil whose work or whose particular extra-curricular activity seems to have exceeded his or her normal performance or to have shown particular devotion, then the Head will inevitably establish a very rich and valuable contact with a vast range of pupils in the school of all ages, abilities and interests. This need not lead to protracted conversations but it certainly affords interesting insights and perceptions. The system of recognition which the Head administers himself and which allows him to praise pupils in a personal way once a week is vital in setting the tone of encouragement. When Wellington was asked what he would do differently if he were to live his life again he replied "I would give more praise." Surely what we as Heads should do most, contrary to the perception of many, is to praise. In order to do so the Head must establish such a system to supplement the informal contacts which extra-curricular activities afford. How often too, in such a relaxed context, the pupil will confide his hopes and fears.

Although many schools, including the day sector, have a Chaplain, it can still be valuable in certain circumstances for a Head to undertake hospital and home visits. Not that the Head's visit to hospital is always appreciated: care must be taken that it is well judged and not likely to lead inadvertently to cardiac arrest in the horrified patient. But there can be in such a context outside school, in circumstances of pain or difficulty, a contact established with a pupil which is invaluable in altering a perception. The home visit or the hospital visit, while it is primarily best and most expectedly undertaken by a Chaplain or Housemaster, can from time to time be a helpful way for a Head to convey the overriding value of concern.

Some Heads, at least until age or arthritis precludes such enthusiasm, find value in coaching games, however gently. This might be cricket or hockey (it would be unwise were it soccer, rugby or judo...) and, particularly with junior pupils, it can provide a means of establishing early contact in an informal context in which the Head may demonstrate overwhelming normality, even deeply reassuring incompetence. Orchestras, plays and choirs offer similar participation and alternative bridges.

When I first began to teach I found it difficult to believe that the Headmaster did anything but umpire hockey and generally wander around. He always seemed to be evident, observing, leaning against a pillar and chatting to pupils. It seemed an admirable way of earning a living. (I was not awake to see his light on at 2 am.) But that, of course, is 25 years ago and things have changed. Some of that subtle policy of deliberately wandering around with no discernible haste or purpose can be profitably retained, even in the metronomic life which Heads tend to lead. The simple question "How's life?" in corridor or quad can be unexpectedly useful. Mostly it will elicit an evasive grunt, sometimes the embarrassed smile. But it may also be the casual key which turns an important lock.

How closely can a Head really know a pupil? Well, there will clearly be circumstances, usually in crisis (bereavement, redundancy, divorce, anxiety, unhappiness), when pupils will choose to refer to the Head, whether there is a Chaplain or not. This will probably be rare but when it occurs the Head must in no circumstances turn away or delegate. By his response he will indicate the real values of the school. Inevitably, though, pupils will turn primarily to form teachers, tutors or Housemasters, depending upon the particular pastoral system in operation, and the Head will be called upon more commonly to administer discipline or advice after considerable consultation has occurred between pupil and teacher. Nevertheless, it seems important that the Head, without in any sense muddying the waters or intervening in a sensitive pastoral structure, should make strenuous efforts through his Chaplain, Housemasters or year tutors to know where the domestic problems lie. In this regard the Head's own secretary, who will in all probability be the first point of contact (certainly in a day school) can apprise him rapidly of domestic or financial problems affecting pupils and it is not difficult for a Head to find a pupil and talk over an issue informally. The balance however between the Head as dispassionate leader of a community and the Head as more personal Housemaster needs to be clear and understood. It is not easy to do so and it is all too easy for a Head to convey one at the expense of the other. Nevertheless, by regular briefing and by informal contact with pupils thereafter, a Head can, through his Housemasters, Heads of Department and Chaplains, learn of potential personal or academic difficulties and address these as he thinks fit. Pupils must know they can turn to the Head and something of that old open door can still survive.

The Head's contact with prefects is also important in establishing a sense of purpose and priorities and in understanding the psychology of the pupils as a whole. But it would be unwise for the Head to be too close to prefects and it is in many senses easier for such administrative contact to be with the Deputy or senior Housemaster. Where the Head will learn most from prefects is what the preoccupations of the young are, where the problem areas are developing, how certain decisions have been viewed, why justice appears not to have been observed, which rules seem unreasonable. However, while some Heads believe that informal social contact through parties and lunches is appropriate with senior pupils such as prefects, great caution must be observed and in a day school it may seem unwise. As with the pupil body as a whole, so with prefects there must be some distance between the Head and the pupils and such occasions may seem artificial. Trial by dinner or tea party is a British affliction, the skill of which is to maintain communication at a superficial level. Neither is really suited to personal understanding. Yet in a natural anxiety to know too much too soon and to establish an air of informality or misguided equality, some Heads initially cultivate excessive closeness to pupils, especially senior pupils, and there is in this policy considerable risk.

The Head should not undervalue the collective address. Although there may be a tendency for pupils to defer their attention at a Monday morning assembly, the formal address by the Head, sparingly used, can be of considerable importance in the perceptions of the school. Indeed it is at assemblies, in Chapel and on public occasions – perhaps Prizegivings or Founder's Days – that the Head can best convey a message or philosophy. Much will be disregarded at the time. But some will be retained. A coherent philosophy for the school has to be conveyed collectively through speeches and through the Head's own perceived example and practice.

The Head is not infrequently called upon to pronounce on some aspect of discipline. This of course he must never shirk but, when individual pupils are referred to him, while discipline must be upheld and standards maintained, the Head must be careful to leave the door open for further consultation with the pupil even when punishment has been firmly administered. How often when one is about to administer punishment does one learn of circumstances which have caused the pupil distress or which may be placing him or her in an impossible domestic situation. It is at times like these that knowledge of the pupil amassed from formal and informal contact, in the classroom, concert hall or quadrangle, is essential.

Above all, despite the conflicting contemporary demands which a Head must meet, it is to my mind in the domain of pastoral care that he or she has most to contribute. This must surely remain the Head's priority in leading a community of young people whose values and attitudes will be shaped for the many years which follow their formal education. Styles of headship may have become less individualistic recently yet still, as the saying goes, the main thing must be to keep the main thing the main thing.

Chapter 7

The Head and the Parents

John Rees

Rector, The Edinburgh Academy

In Summer 1992 national newspapers carried articles about the perils of headship. They pointed to the emergence of parent power as a threat to the supposed inpregnability of he or she who must be obeyed (or at least would have been in the past!). If these articles were to be believed, and if they truly reflected the experience and likely future for Heads, then few would be foolish enough to raise their heads above the ramparts, however great their ambition and lust for power. Any newly-appointed Head must inevitably be concerned about parent power in its various forms and would be unwise to ignore it either in the early days of his or her headship or to become complacent about it as the years roll by. However, as with all potential threats, it is important to see every problem as a challenge, as an opportunity and is a spur to produce the best of which one is capable as an individual and as an institution.

The root of the concern lies in the love-hate relationship between parents and schools. It is as dangerous to generalise about schools as it is about the parents. Parents essentially wish their children to be happy and successful. By the same token they would like their children's schools to be happy and successful and to have good relationships with the teachers as individuals and the school as a whole. However the potential for discontent, strife and misunderstanding is considerable.

Parents are not always consistent. Their reactions may represent a confused response to ambition, unrealistic hopes and deep-seated recognition of the limits of their children. They may also display a lethal mixture of ignorance, knowledge and prejudice. But if we treat them as time-bombs waiting to go off, or merely as the biological and financial agents necessary to provide us with pupils, then we deserve most of the parental problems which arise and which may come to bedevil the life of the Head. Time spent with parents, as individuals or in groups, is rarely wasted. The Head who groans inwardly at the sight of parents, wherever they appear, and seeks to walk 'on the other side' does so at the peril of his or her professional life. Indeed, one might argue that any Head who sees 'parents' as potentially or actually a nuisance has only two options: to find a more appropriate career or a total change of attitude. Twelve years of Headship have taught me, sometimes the hard way, that it is essential to develop and maintain the best of relationships with parents. As with Governors, staff, pupils, press and any other important groups in the life of your school, it is sensible to take the initiative rather than become defensive as the problems roll in.

From the first enquiry to the last farewell parents matter. They bring us their children, pay fees, can support our schools in many ways, and their good opinion is plainly vitally important if we are to sustain our schools over the years. I have always thought it important to write to parents who request a prospectus with as personal a letter as may be possible with the limited information sometimes available, not because I distrust secretaries or registrars but because parents do like the personal touch from the man at the top. Similarly I try to make myself available to parents who telephone and certainly to those who visit, partly because it is an opportunity to sell, partly because I can learn a good deal about them and their children and the relationships between them. This will stand me in good stead in future years. Even if they don't send their children, or we don't accept them, it is important that they should think well of our school and those who run it.

Visiting parents are often surprisingly nervous, frequently making references to "the last time I was in the Headmaster's study", or almost tongue-tied at the thought of now being on equal terms with this daunting figure of authority who has so much potential for good in the life of their child.

Two developments in recent years have strengthened the parental arm. The Parents' Charter has outlined the duties and obligations of the school and the rights of the parent. It has perhaps not been as strong as it should have on the duties and obligations of the parent and the rights of the school. This is complemented by increasing emphasis on the publication of examination results and the introduction of standardised testing at other stages in a child's career. There are those who have sought to pretend that these changes are not afoot and to bury their mortar boards in the sand in the hope that their pursuers will go away. This will not happen.

If we look at the process as an opportunity to examine our own operations more closely and to communicate with parents more effectively, then our school will be a better place and our job an easier and happier one. If we view parents as equal partners in the community then we are more likely, much more likely, to have their full support. I suggest the following checklist to which you will no doubt add your own ideas. Don't be afraid to glean ideas from other colleagues.

Be open and welcoming from the start.

Look at your prospectus from a parent's point of view.

Make any school visit or open day as welcoming as possible.

Sell your strengths but don't try to hide areas which you think need to be improved.

Make sure that the reporting system reports on individuals in a way that makes sense to parents.

Always be willing to talk to parents face-to-face or over the 'phone. If you are not available, make sure that a knowledgeable colleague speaks to the parents and return the call yourself if there are loose ends.

Look for ways of getting to know individual children, and make sure that you write to parents about anything out of the ordinary which the child has achieved. This ensures that when problems arise you are seen in the past to have given due praise to match present complaints.

Develop all possible techniques of getting to know parents, and avoid giving the impression that they are a nuisance.

Make surveys of parental opinion – whole school, year groups, *etc.* Don't rely simply on anecdotal evidence that parents are satisfied; the unhappy may not communicate without some prompting.

Use all obvious means of communication – Speech Days, newsletters or whatever.

Finally, try to put yourself in the place of the parent. Some years ago I wrote the following for a parents' guide to good schools. The suggestions I make to parents complement those I make to Heads – it would be unfortunate if they didn't.

'Do read the prospectus carefully immediately before you visit – don't waste time on covering old ground. Be prepared to talk about hopes and realities, difficulties and concerns. Be willing to accept that, hard as we try, we are not perfect. Don't try to box us into corners which make us claim to be omnipotent and omniscient. Only fools or charlatans would claim to be either, and I doubt whether such a person would be a good Head! As you tour the school, remember that we are not a trade exhibition or a production line – we are a community of people, living and working together, warts and all.

John Rees: "Twelve years of headship have taught me, sometimes the hard way, that it is essential to maintain and develop the best of relationships with parents."

'Don't be frightened to ask "silly" questions. If they matter to you, then ask them. Don't despair if your child interviews badly. However relaxed we try to make it, this is a very daunting experience for him or her. We do make allowances. As you build up a picture of us from different sources, so we too build our view based on what we talk about and from our contacts with junior schools. Do be honest about your visits to other schools; and ultimately do be honest about which school is your first choice.

'Don't be bemused by facilities and exam results. Facilities are only as good as the use to which they are put by all members of the community. Exam results reflect both the ability of pupils and staff and issues such as entry policy. Judicious withdrawal of weak candidates may not do much for the candidate but can do wonders for percentage pass rates! Most parents are concerned for the whole child. This is the most difficult thing to assess on a visit but it is surely the most important. Make sure that you meet the current pupils if at all possible.'

Headship must be the most exciting job in the world because of its variety and because we are working for the future of children. Enjoy working with their parents too!

Chapter 8

The Head and Former Pupils

Hugh Monro
Headmaster, Clifton College

It is said that there are three key issues in American education. For the students it is sex, for the teachers parking and for the alumni sports results. Whilst we all have had experience of some of these problems the alumni's interest is usually expressed less emphatically in Britain.

There is confusion in British schools about the role of Old Boys and Old Girls (hereafter Old Boys). The fear of a reactionary force opposed to change, which sees the school as it was and allows that sepia-coloured view to stop any significant alterations, is usually exaggerated. Old Boys do not all have similar memories of their school. Many will want no contact at all. Most will have detailed knowledge of only five years of the school and little contact with other age groups. A grandfather, a father and son or daughter may all have attended the same school, and even the same house, but have completely contrasting attitudes.

Nevertheless former pupils are a source of many things which can benefit the school – among them finance, development, contacts, careers, influence, information and of course as providers of another generation of pupils. So any new Head must establish early in his or her tenure what role the OBs will play. Is it to be a relationship based on fund-raising? If so will it be counter-productive? Many appeals suffer from amateur organization, whilst others fail because professional fund-raisers know little or nothing of the school's traditions or ethos. Can the Head be involved productively?

Most families now receive literature appealing for money from an ever- increasing range of charities. Schools must compete with overseas disasters, churches, hospitals and many local good causes. The old school is not an easy cause to promote against these. Fund-raising is unlikely to achieve the role that it now plays in American schools. There, with a different tax system and a tradition of giving, it is an established and vital part of every school's financial base that endowment enrichment campaigns should be annual drives. All alumni are expected to contribute and a full-time self-funding administration ensures that they do.

Yet relations with Old Boys and Old Girls can be so much more. Regional dinners allow a network to be created and age-based reunions allow links to be re-established. If a Head goes to a variety of these events a much more balanced view of the school will emerge. What really happened in the 1940s and what the now established and staid pillar of the Common Room was like as a young inexperienced teacher is extremely useful information. So too is the response of those present to proposed changes. Some of them can be very useful in providing support and acting as sounding boards.

Yet one of the most tempting mistakes is to imagine that all those present see themselves primarily

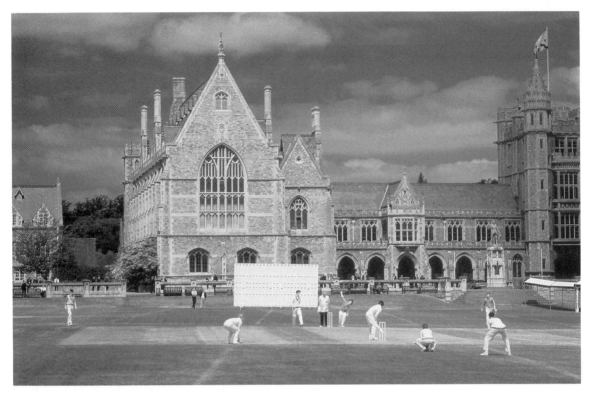

Clifton College: "A grandfather, a father and son or daughter may all have attended the same school, and even the same house, but have completely contrasting attitudes".

as former pupils. They are, first, usually successful in their own careers. Secondly they are usually family members with children and grandchildren of their own. These are the two really significant factors.

A well-kept and up-to-date list of occupations should be one of the most useful aids to a careers department. Few Old Boys will not be prepared to give advice to individual pupils interested in specific professions. Successful entrepreneurs and industrialists must be allowed to influence boys and girls. Can the Old Boys' Society organize a presentation by ten or a dozen of its members, who are now in their thirties and launched into successful careers?

Similarly this list will be most useful to the school authorities. Advice from experts can be sought informally. If a stamp collection is left to the school, an Old Boy may be able to suggest the best way of selling it. If it is to be kept and displayed, is there an Old Boy who specialises in mounting exhibitions? Expertise is available and should be called upon.

This same expertise should be available to the Governors. I suspect that Old Boys make the best and worst Governors. Those who have moved on to successful careers will, however busy, be able to bring their expertise to bear on the school's problems. Medical, legal and financial advice can be obtained from many institutions and individuals but an Old Boy who feels he owes his school a debt will be a great source of sensible advice. A Head can talk openly about the weaknesses of his school with someone who has been a pupil there.

However it is important that Old Boys on the governing body are balanced by other groups. Successful role models for girl pupils are vital in the early years of coeducation; they cannot have been educated at the school. Similarly, if a senior member of staff has taught most of the Governors, he may well be able to wield significant power. There is no ideal quota, but a balance is needed. A governing body solely of Old Boys is likely to be inward-looking and reactionary; one with none is likely to be insensitive to the school's tradition.

Former pupils at a school are also potential parents. The Old Boys' Society should inform all of them of what is happening at the school and in particular there should be a strong message to the 30-40 year olds. Several schools produce a magazine solely for Old Boys who are prospective parents. Although there is a risk of it being a bland catalogue of successes, anything which keeps the school in the minds of 30 and 40 year olds must be productive.

The success of the Old Boys' Society depends on its secretary. Too many schools see the post as a sinecure for a retired Housemaster and assume that it will work smoothly. In fact, the job has two specific roles. The administration needs to be ruthlessly efficient. Information about remembering the school in a will must not be sent to the wrong P R Smith. Nor must the just-out-of-prison A J Jones be asked to contribute to a careers convention. A deep knowledge of the school and its characters is invaluable and will help the Head enormously.

But there is more to it than that. Old Boys expect a friendly welcome when they call in. They want someone who can organize dinners and reunions so that they meet old friends. They want anecdotes and shared memories. The secretary has a vital role to play but he mustn't be too powerful or the Society can become dominated by one age group. Recent leavers don't want the Society over-whelmed by the over-70s, the Masons or the Golf Society. The secretary's job is to ensure that the balance is kept and that no Old Boy feels the Society belongs to others.

The most annoying phenomenon is the 'professional Old Boy'. He will appear at all sorts of occasions decked in buttons, cuff-links and tie, all of which show his loyalty. He will usually hover on the edge of a group before pouncing and beginning his tirade. It is vital to deal firmly but politely with him as he will have limpet-like tenacity. Only by doing this will the Head have time to talk to as many Old Boys as possible. A reunion of an age group can be an opportunity to talk to 20 or 30 completely dissimilar people. It is vital not to spend all the time with the bishop or the successful banker. The enjoyment of the occasion is in the extraordinary range of careers and experiences gathered around one table.

The school does not belong to the Old Boys but then it does not belong to the present Head, staff and pupils either. Their 15, 30 and 5 years are only short chapters in the school's full story. Nevertheless no Head sensibly ignores his Old Boys' Society. Former pupils are a source of strength. They need attention and time. Their support is vital in many ways – not solely financial – and a school-based organization which helps them is vital. Every occasion where they gather is a fertile place in which to spread the good news of the school's progress and every Head should return from such events having talked to a wide variety of normal and interesting people and ready to deal with...the parking issue.

Chapter 9

The Head
and the Governors

Roger Griffiths

*Membership Secretary, The Headmasters' Conference and
formerly Headmaster, Hurstpierpoint College*

"A cynic on receiving these guidelines for Governors may well murmur 'a good Governor does not need them: a poor Governor will probably not read them'." So says the admirable *Guidelines for Governors* produced by The Association of Governing Bodies of Public Schools and Association of Governing Bodies of Girls' Public Schools. In fact the whole document contains immensely valuable advice. If only all Governors both read the contents and went along with the code of conduct it contains, there would be far fewer problems for Heads and far less upheaval in the scholastic world.

It is stating the obvious that the post of Head is a lonely one. Within the confines of the school the most important people whose support is absolutely vital from the Head's point of view are, in my opinion, the Bursar, the Second Master and the Chaplain. In most schools the appointment of at least two, and sometimes all three, of these is usually made either by the governing body with the agreement of the Head, or by the Head with the agreement of the governing body. These key appointments are a joint matter and this must always be borne in mind.

The Head must have confidence in his management team and they of course must have confidence in him. When there is a breakdown of relations on either side it is the duty and prime function of the Governors, and particularly of the Chairman, to mediate. But their prime responsibility is to the Head whom they have chosen. All of them, including the Head, owe complete allegiance to the school. Therefore it follows that the most important function of the Governors is to choose the right Head for the school and then to provide full support. All Governors, and particularly the Chairman, must be prepared to give that support in public even if they disagree with the Head, or agree to differ, in private. In no way do I imply that the Head should be in sole control and allowed to get away with whatever he likes. On the other hand he does need to know that at all times there is someone to whom he can turn for advice. Therefore above everything else the Chairman must be a good listener. If disagreements grow then the situation becomes more difficult. But in essence the Chairman and his fellow Governors can make or break a Head and therefore a school.

Procedures for choosing a Head, including the role to be played by the present incumbent, are very clearly and fully set out in *Guidelines for Governors*. The procedures may vary from one school to another but it is important that in the final choice there should be unanimity amongst the whole governing body. It is essential also that neither the present Head's authority is undermined nor the future incumbent pre-judged by staff. Occasional thoughtlessness does not help. On one occasion a governing body about to appoint a new Head quite correctly invited those on the short list to come and look at the school. They also invited them to meet the members of the Common Room. At this point things went astray, for the Governors invited the Common Room to vote as to which of the candidates they would like to have as Head. When the final selection was made the Common Room had voted for one candidate and Governors appointed another. This was not a sure recipe for success.

Although the appointment of a new Head is the most important role for the Governors the Chairman carries the ultimate responsibility. It is for him or her to set up the selection committee and to outline the responsibilities and duties of the incoming Head. At the same time, even at the early stage of the preliminary interviews, the impression must be given to candidates that the governing body is there to support the Head at all times. As it says in *Guidelines for Governors*, the relation between a governing body and its Head should be one of complete trust with unfettered frankness of discussion and a generous recognition by the governing body that the Head has full freedom of operation in the discharge of his or her responsibilities. Within full frankness of discussion however it must be made clear that when Governors receive criticism of a Head, the Head must always be given a chance to put his side of the story. It is wrong for Governors to act merely on the complaints of disaffected staff or disappointed parents without giving the Head a chance to show that the criticisms are unfounded.

In connection with a Head having full freedom of operation in the discharge of responsibilities, one of my main tasks – and one of the most important ones – is to check over with the Head the contract he has been offered to ensure that his position is secure and the various procedures are fair and satisfactory. The main sections which I study are those concerned with dismissal. When this occurs it is particularly important that the correct procedure is gone through. There is a splendid model contract drawn up by GBA and HMC a few years ago to help Governors. In all such matters it is vital that justice is seen to be done and the key phrase deals with the number of Governors concerned with the dismissal procedures. It is vital that every Governor should have a vote, even if he or she cannot be present at the meeting in question. It is very right that all our members should be given every support and protection by the Conference as well as by their Governors. Although as Membership Secretary of this 'trade union' it is my duty to support members to the full, nevertheless I do on occasions have a sneaking sympathy with the governing body because of the way a Head may have behaved, however unwittingly.

I have never liked the assumption that a school is a business, that the Chairman is the chairman of the board and that the Head is the managing director whose head must fall if results are bad, numbers are dropping and finances under pressure. This has been described as the 'Football Manager Syndrome'. One Headmaster was confronted by his Chairman of Governors (a successful business-man) when numbers in the school were going down and the finances were a little shaky. "In my business," said the Chairman, "when you cannot market your product and the finances are in the red there is one man responsible, the Chief Executive, and you get rid of him as quickly as possible. Therefore, Headmaster, I feel that it would be to the school's advantage if you were to leave next

Roger Griffiths: "I have never liked the assumption that a school is a business".

summer". What he failed to realise was that a new Head can induce more apprehension amongst local parents and prep school Heads until he has established himself than a Headmaster in situ who over the years has won their respect.

To me a school cannot be compared with any other aspect of society. Within it those who are ultimately responsible are the Head and the Chairman who need to be frequently, though not necessarily always, in touch. I do not mean to imply that all decisions should be taken in advance of Governors' meetings by the Head and the Chairman, but it is very important to have clear ideas to put before a group of men and women who may not have as much time to spend on the affairs of the school as the Head does and the Chairman must.

The ways of Chairmen are sometimes mysterious. My first Chairman would stay the night before the Governors' meeting. We would go through the whole agenda working out what decisions should be taken. He would then spend the morning of the meeting moving the mood of those present in diametrically the opposite direction from that which we had agreed the previous night. After lunch, he would skilfully lead them back to the original decisions! He did confess to me after one such meeting that there was nothing he enjoyed more than manipulating people. It was certainly a swift way of giving a Head a gastric ulcer, and there are plenty of ways of achieving that without acquiring one from your Chairman of Governors as well!

The word which crops up more frequently than any other when there are criticisms either of the Head or of the governing body is 'communication'. A Head, however scholarly or successful in the world of education, may not necessarily be good at communicating with staff. This is where the Chairman and all Governors can help, or the opposite. It is essential however that a Head is always given a chance to put his side of the story informally before any formal Governors' meetings take place.

I recall one school where the Governors met with the Headmaster in the morning. They had, as the Head thought, a successful meeting and lunch together. The Governors then left the school but went to a local hotel where they considered various complaints which had been made about the Headmaster by members of staff. None had been mentioned to the Head at any time. At five o'clock the Chairman and Vice-Chairman returned to the Head's study and said that they had just had a meeting and had decided that he should leave the School the following July. This to a man who had been in his second Headship for a number of years. Whether or not the criticisms were justified, as a matter of good practice the Head should have been given a chance to put his side of the story informally.

Every year there are disputes between governing bodies and their Heads which might have been avoided had they followed a key passage in the introduction to *Guidelines for Governors*. It points out in particular that the most important functions of a governing body are, apart from the appointment of a Head, ultimate responsibility for the educational policy and the control of finance. Therefore all Governors must be fully aware of what is going on in the school. It is the Chairman's duty not only to be fully aware of everything himself but to ensure that, as far as possible, the other members are active and not passive. Incidentally there is an interesting section in *Guidelines for Governors* about the composition of a governing body with emphasis on the value of having former members of the school but not in excessive numbers.

It is a good thing that there should be a couple of former parents – not current parents for obvious reasons – and there is value in having an age limit for Governors. I recall visiting one school where a young member of staff asked me if I could help as a visiting Governor had forgotten his own name. This was not an April Fool. The elderly gentleman in question had genuinely forgotten who he was and, when I managed to remember his name and he was told, we had to pin it on him in case he forgot it again! If a Governor reaches 70 but is still quite clearly of considerable value to the deliberations of the governing body then one can always use co-option.

Every Governor will wish to make a contribution so it is vital that he or she regularly attends Governors' meetings and as many other school functions as possible. It is important to get to know members of staff and their families – domestic and ground as well as teaching staff. Pupils also should not merely dismiss Governors as (in the words of one schoolgirl) "that group of wrinklies who come down once a term, have a good lunch, put up the fees and go away again!" Governors should also know the school buildings and plant and be aware of the accommodation and any problems therein. The governing body should have on it people with a wide variety of interests and abilities, again very obvious. Above all, the Governors should ensure that they have not only the right Head but also the right Chairman.

In what ways then can a Chairman and his fellow Governors really help a Head? First, by being, I repeat, a good listener; secondly by being prepared to spend a considerable amount of time on the school's affairs; thirdly by taking a personal interest in the Head and his family and making sure that spouse and children are not neglected or a wife over-burdened. Although a good Head will wish to devote himself completely to his School, as indeed may his wife, it is vital that they have some family existence as well. It is only the Governors who can really tell them that. I do not necessarily mean the provision of a sabbatical break every so often, but more a discreet surveillance of what goes on.

In the past it was only too often taken for granted by Governors, and indeed by many of those in the school, that the Headmaster's wife was prepared to sacrifice herself completely for the school. Indeed the assumption was also that the Headmaster was prepared to sacrifice his family for it as well. Now most governing bodies take a more sensible attitude. If a wife has a profession of her own which she wishes to follow, providing she also manages to find time to take part in school activities, that is accepted as perfectly valid. At the same time there are still many wives who wish to devote themselves entirely to the school and one can only hope that governing bodies make appropriate recognition of this. So far as family life goes, it is essential that the Governors should impress upon the Head that he must, however devoted he is to the school, devote also as much time as possible to his family and to maintaining contact with people outside the school.

In an excellent article in *The Times* (August 1992) Baroness Warnock argued that market forces are diminishing education. She was writing in particular about the resignation of a Headmistress from a leading girls' school. In her article she was saddened by the fact that the governing body had listened to parents' criticisms and the press rather than back a Head with imagination and vision. Baroness Warnock's argument was that the market is essentially conservative. She reasoned that parents are not looking for excellence or educational imaginativeness but merely for examination success. Her conclusion was, sadly, that if market forces cause bad schools to wither away then the risk remains that what is left will be uniformly safe, neither bad nor good.

At present there is a national decline in boarding numbers. Governors who are responsible amongst other things for the financial viability of the school may look with some distress when numbers and finances are down. However it is not the Head alone, the registrar alone, or indeed the teaching staff alone who can be held responsible. To react to such a situation as though it were the business world, and get rid of the 'chief executive' in the hope that a new one may provide more satisfactory financial results, will not necessarily be the right solution. Nearly every school will from time to time have a bad year for academic results. No school should be judged on one year's results alone. Every school, particularly boarding schools, will suffer a drop in numbers from time to time. Again this should be looked at in the long and not the short term. Most schools go through a period of popularity and a period when public taste and choice move elsewhere. All must be looked at in the long term. It is no good blaming a Head for immediate and sudden and passing failures, and it is up to all Governors to take a long term view however worrying the immediate situation is.

In the present economic climate it is important for a Head to take a part in the life of the community and in the educational world at large. It is essential that the Governors give every backing and support in this, enabling him to be absent from the school at times and understanding when absences may seem to be more frequent.

I mentioned earlier how important it is that the Head should be on good terms with his management team. A key figure in this is the Bursar. The position of Bursar varies greatly from school to school, but broadly he looks after the financial and property management and the efficient operation of all ancillary services. In some cases the Bursar is responsible directly to the governing body and in others to the Head, but good personal relationships are essential in order that everything may proceed well in the school. In some cases the Bursar is also clerk to the Governors. This can have clear advantages as well as disadvantages and it is essential that upon appointment a Head is put fully in the picture. If the Governors tend to rely too much on the clerk as their source of information about the running of the school then there are bound to be problems; the position of the Head is endangered and good relations and communication may suffer. After all, it is the Head who is ultimately responsible for everything that happens in the school though usually he is only too happy to leave much of the day to day running to his management team. It is vital that the Governors ensure that the Head has a full say in the appointment of the Bursar, as indeed in the appointment of other senior staff if they are the responsibility of the governing body.

Nowadays I find an increasing number of occasions where a Head and Governors are finding difficulties working together. It saddens me that colleagues and former colleagues have been placed in situations by their governing bodies in which long service and good conduct seem to have been ignored in the face of adverse criticisms, adverse publicity, the present political and financial climate or indeed merely a result of a clash of personalities. Governors today have to play an increasingly vital role in the running of a school whilst at the same time ensuring that the Head is left freedom of movement.

With the state schools evolving their system of Governors it is time for all our school governing bodies to take a long hard look at themselves and the way in which they function. The Governing Bodies Association is fully aware of this and has begun a series of one-day seminars for Chairmen of Governors and also for new Governors. It is no longer a one-sided process whereby someone will lend their name or title to the appropriate page in the prospectus. Governors have to be aware of what is going on in education, what it is like to be involved in the day-to-day running of a school, of the at times claustrophobic atmosphere of a school in the ninth or tenth week of a long hard term. When the governing body is behind the Head and when he has the confidence of them, his staff, parents and pupils, then the sky is the limit. Despite all problems in the present day running of schools they can still be the best of all possible worlds. It is up to Governors and Heads to see that they remain so.

Most of our governing bodies consist of people who above everything else have the good of the school at heart. That is the most important aspect I would like to stress. To the Head of course his school and career are the most important. At the same time, inevitably, a Head may have a particular and sometimes, I fear, narrow view of the situation. A Head needs to look at the wider implications and it is for the Governors to advise him on this.

I would not wish to give the impression that there is a great deal wrong in our schools. In most Heads are running very good establishments with the full and complete support of their governing bodies, staff, parents and pupils. This should apply to all our schools. To ensure that that is the case I commend every Governor and every Head who reads this to study (if not for the first time) *Guidelines for Governors*, a document which sums up all that is best to ensure the prosperity of the schools which we serve and the people who work in them.

Chapter 10

Marketing your School

Graham Able

Headmaster, Hampton School

It is widely accepted in industry that one can only market effectively a good product which fulfils a perceived need. The most essential factors in marketing a school are therefore to formulate clearly its aims and objectives, establish that these are in accordance with the wishes of likely prospective parents and then to ensure that the school is successful in achieving them.

Proof of this effectiveness can be difficult for the more subjective aims but academic league tables, here to stay whether we approve or not, have encouraged prospective parents to expect some evidence for everything that a school claims to achieve. They are making a considerable investment in their children's education and they expect them to gain tangible advantages from the outlay. Nearly all parents will anticipate an increased chance of academic success, but other factors will also be important – leadership, cultural and sporting opportunities *etc* – and the individual ethos of a particular school is often vital in determining their final choice.

The ethos must therefore be carefully identified. It should be reflected in the aims and objectives and clearly understood by all staff, pupils and parents. Although many establishments take such an understanding for granted, I suggest that a short statement of aims and objectives (a 'mission statement' in marketing jargon) should be incorporated into the prospectus and issued separately to the staff. It is vital that all the staff understand and are sympathetic towards what the school is trying to achieve, and it is helpful if they can communicate this clearly to any prospective parents or pupils.

Its ethos should be reflected in the school's corporate image. There is no excuse, given the ready availability of modern word-processing packages, for sloppy presentation of any written material. The school crest, in the same format, should be on all official notepaper and it should also be on any internal memoranda forms. This gives a consistent image to the public and reinforces a sense of corporate identity within the school. Similarly there are powerful arguments for having the crest on all exercise books, the school hymn book and minibuses. Some would argue against naming the last at all, but I would argue that school vehicles should be seen as an opportunity for free advertising – a view which should also help to ensure their proper maintenance and cleanliness.

All communications by letter to parents, prospective parents and feeder schools should be in keeping with the school's ethos and ideally be in an accepted 'house style'. This can only be achieved if the Head or a senior member of staff reads such letters before they are sent. This is not such an onerous task as it may seem: many letters rapidly become standardised and it is surely preferable to spend a few minutes checking what has been written before it is posted than to take considerably longer trying to repair the damage afterwards.

Graham Able: ". . . one can only market effectively a good product which fulfils a perceived need".

The first contact with most prospective parents is by telephone, usually to the Head's office, and all schools must recognise the importance of this to their marketing effort. It is essential that all the secretarial staff have pleasant, welcoming and helpful telephone manners, and a set form of greeting can be an aid to achieving this as well as giving a stronger image of the school. This should be thoroughly discussed with the secretarial staff who should be aware of their importance in marketing their school and maintaining its good public image. If a prospective parent receives a curt and unhelpful response from the school office, he or she is unlikely to believe your claims that the school is extremely caring towards its pupils.

The initial telephone call is most often to request a copy of the school's prospectus, and this is a major marketing tool which every new Head should review sooner rather than later. Most schools opt to have their prospectus produced for them by outside specialists, but I would question the wisdom of this. Whereas it is obviously right to present the school in its best light, I feel that it is important that the prospectus accurately reflects the ethos and life of the school. I would therefore suggest that the text and layout should be done by a team of staff under the direction of the Head. It can be desktop published 'in house' and then printed professionally. Because such a production is always likely to be more individual and more characteristic of the school, it should attract only those prospective parents who are in sympathy with its aims. This should in turn lead to a higher ratio of registrations per visit and therefore a more productive use of the Head's time.

There is however a caveat. Although any good school should have teaching staff skilled in both writing text and formulating layouts, very few will have the luxury of a professional photographer in their employ. So I strongly recommend that one is hired and carefully briefed if photographs are to be included, as even the keenest amateur is likely to produce less than satisfactory results. Whether you actually require photographs – which date very quickly – in your prospectus is another matter: I would question their necessity in a day school as any parents wishing to consider it will by definition live close enough to come to see for themselves. But this would not always be true of a boarding school where photographs may therefore be more desirable.

Schools develop and evolve quite rapidly, and it is essential that a prospectus should reflect the establishment as it is and is likely to be over the coming five or seven years – not as it was five or even ten years ago. I thus prefer to reprint the prospectus yearly, as do all universities and Oxbridge colleges, with (often minor) textual changes, but it would undoubtedly be quite expensive to have new photographs on an annual basis. Herein lies the dilemma, as photographs featuring pupils date very rapidly but those devoid of pupils tend to give a rather undynamic image to the school. Whatever your decision on photographs, do give careful attention to the prospectus and ensure that it fully reflects the school and its strengths.

When it goes out to prospective parents the prospectus should be accompanied by a letter from the Headmaster. This is your chance to reflect the ethos of the school and to set the tone for all future correspondence with the parents. It is also a very powerful factor in the marketing process. Although the letter will naturally be a standardised one, it should certainly be personalized – word processors have allowed us to become much more professional in our marketing skills – and signed in ink by you. In addition to this letter, I think that it is now essential to enclose details of the previous year's academic and other results. If you do not, prospective parents will wonder what you are trying to hide, and you can always include appropriate comments if you wish. I favour publishing academic and sporting results together with a list of major concerts and plays without further comment.

How does one deal with prospective parents when they visit the school? I strongly recommend that you let sixth formers show them round the school first and then allow them 30 minutes of your time after the tour has finished. If you feel that you cannot entrust the first task to your sixth formers with every expectation of their doing it very well then marketing is probably the least of your worries! My experience is that even the least likely ones promote their school in a most positive manner and are highly effective salesmen.

It is undoubtedly important that all prospective parents should have the opportunity to meet the Head. You personify the school for them. They will often have some questions for you although most will have already been answered by the sixth former, but they will at least want to check whether you really have two heads, and the more discerning will probably probe your attitude to discipline, delinquency and drugs. The prospective parents' response to the school, and to their interview with you, will not only help to determine whether their son or daughter is then registered but it will also be communicated to others who may in turn be potential prospective parents. Heads should never forget that other people's impressions of them will be widely communicated and be an important factor in the marketing of their school.

Why do prospective parents make contact in the first place? There are three likely sources of information: word of mouth from present or past parents or pupils, a recommendation from a feeder school Head, or an advertisement or article in the local or national media.

I strongly suspect that the first source is by far the most important. Thus the most effective marketing is to ensure good relationships with parents and past pupils. In this respect marketing one's school resembles marketing any other service – a satisfied customer provides the most effective advertising. Regular reunions for former pupils and social events for current parents, in addition to the necessary close liaison over their offsprings' progress, can thus be seen to have important claims on any marketing budget. The influence of preparatory school Heads should never be underestimated however and time spent building good relationships here is time very well spent. I prefer to invite feeder school Heads to luncheon on an individual basis and use such occasions to ensure that contacts

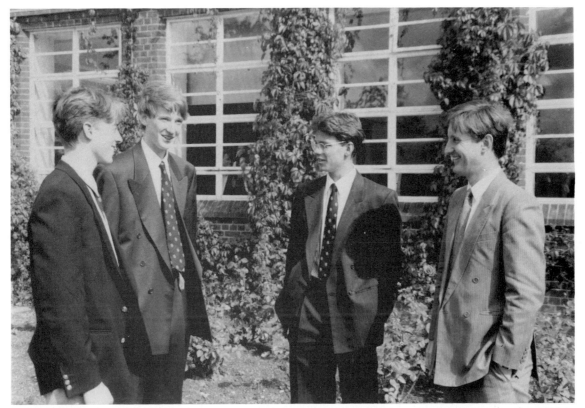

"The most effective marketing agents are satisfied clients - the parents of current and former pupils and those pupils themselves".

are maintained not only with me but also with other key senior staff. It is equally important to accept, wherever possible, invitations to preparatory speech days and their increasingly popular evening seminars on senior schools. An honest partnership with preparatory schools on what you will accept at Common Entrance helps to ensure that any marketing done by them on your behalf is effective and does not waste time: an apparently full list which produces several failures does nobody credit, but you also rapidly lose credibility if you claim to require a mark 10% higher than you will actually accept.

I suspect that media advertising is less effective in attracting pupils than the media would wish us to believe, but much depends on the type of school and the cost effectiveness of reaching the right people. Day schools usually find that advertising for 11-plus or sixth form entrance examinations in the local press is a profitable exercise, but there is little to be said for taking expensive space in national colour supplements. Boarding schools would normally expect the reverse to be true, but they should be careful to identify their catchment before parting with considerable sums of money. On the other hand all schools may want to make use of the rather less expensive Court Circular columns to publicise scholarships or other events and hence advertise somewhat more subtly.

Of course any favourable (or even moderately critical) free publicity is excellent for marketing, and regular press releases – at least to the local media – are well worth the effort even if the school only gets a mention one week in five. Even more care needs to be taken with the press however than with correspondence to parents, and Heads should always check carefully anything given to the media.

Videos are becoming increasingly popular and may, I would suggest, solve the dilemma regarding prospectuses and photographs. It is realistic and not prohibitively expensive to produce a new school video every two or three years and to use this to complement written material. Prospective parents and most certainly prospective pupils are increasingly more used to gaining information via the television screen than from the written word, and thus a good school video can be a powerful marketing tool.

Amateur videos, however well produced, are likely to look somewhat substandard. I would strongly urge all Heads who wish to use this medium for marketing purposes to employ a professional company with a good reputation. Once again however it is vital that the school should have the final say over the editing in order that the finished product should give a true feeling of life at the school. Videos can be particularly useful as a general introduction to school life on open days.

Open days fall broadly into two categories: those that would seek to portray the school on a normal working day and show a large number of prospective parents classes, games, and other activities taking place 'as usual', and the more presentational type of open day (usually either an evening or a Saturday afternoon) when the many activities of the school are on display accompanied by concerts, plays and sporting fixtures, but with classes not in session. I suspect that the first type may be more immediately effective in marketing the school, but the second type is extremely popular with current parents. As the relationship with current parents is in itself a very important marketing tool there is perhaps a case for both types of open day occurring during the school year. With either format it is possible to have a formal address from the Headmaster at some stage in the proceedings, but this will depend on a more regimented approach than may be desirable if the school is expecting to attract a very large number of visitors over a period of several hours. Prospective parents may additionally be invited to specified school events, but this presupposes that they have already been identified and that there is room to accommodate them. Such invitations may be more effectively directed to Heads of feeder schools.

It is possible to employ marketing consultants to help with prospectuses, videos, open days and any other aspects of the school's marketing policy. In many cases this may be a cost effective and useful exercise, although my experience has been that there is usually enough marketing expertise amongst the staff of a good school provided that the expertise is both well motivated and well directed. Certainly if the Head is considering an outside marketing consultant, he or she should first ensure that the consultant has a good track record, has something to offer which cannot be provided from within and is therefore worth the considerable fees which will probably be charged. Some are very good, but it must be realised that there are many who have little to offer. Marketing courses for senior staff may be a better use of the school budget.

To sum up, the most important aspect of marketing is to make sure that the school is demonstrably achieving its aims; this can only be done if the staff is properly focused and committed. The socio-economic and geographic catchments should be clearly identified and targeted. Appropriate media coverage and advertising can then make a useful and cost-effective contribution to the marketing of a school, but liaison with feeder schools is considerably more important and should be nurtured carefully. The most effective marketing agents however are satisfied clients – the parents of current and former pupils and those pupils themselves. The better a school looks after its clients the less ancillary marketing it will have to provide for itself.

Chapter 11

The Head and Academic Development

Vivian Anthony

*Secretary, The Headmasters' Conference and formerly
Headmaster of Colfe's School, London*

Even if there was not a current obsession with publishing examination results and composing league tables showing schools' comparative academic performances, few Heads would not put academic goals high on the list of priorities. While most Heads have a much broader idea of what constitutes a good education than simply high grades in external examinations, there is no doubt that most parents and Governors expect schools to perform great feats, if not miracles, in this area.

Hopefully the Head and the management team will be willing and able to adopt a liberal and enlightened educational philosophy which will support 'a broad and balanced curriculum' (Education Reform Act 1988) as well as aiming high in exams. In practice these two goals are as often in competition as they are complementary. How often will you hear from a Head of Department that if only he could have two more teaching periods a week he could improve the results, whereas you were about to suggest a cut of one period in his allocation so that information technology could be taught more effectively. However the right signals must be given if the academic life of the school is to have high priority that must be reflected in your decisions when there are clashes over pupils' time.

One advantage of the early appointment of Heads – few have less than two terms to prepare – is that they can make some analysis of the health of the academic departments of the school before taking over. Most outgoing Heads will have a clear idea of strengths and weaknesses and what they would have wanted to do had they been staying. Other senior colleagues are usually happy to give their opinions, some of which can be checked against performance in external examinations in recent years. Such preparation is essential if the early meetings with individual Heads of Department are to be effective. It would be wise to give careful thought to their suggestions for improving their departments and to consider the future of those who have no suggestions. They may have comments about the strengths and weaknesses of members of their department and these thoughts may be a valuable starting point in the discussions (appraisal) you will be having with them later. The arrival of a new Head is the ideal time for a renewed search for solutions to problems in academic departments which may have been evident for some time.

Many of the problems will not be new to the incoming Head, although it may not have been his particular responsibility to deal with them in the past unless as a Director of Studies this had been expected. Those problems which arise from inadequate facilities are usually easier dealt with than those from inadequate teachers. Besides we have all experienced outstanding teaching carried out in poor buildings with the minimum of equipment. Nevertheless this is the starting point for a development plan aimed at improving the conditions under which teachers and pupils can strive for the highest academic goals.

Such development is the subject of the following. The role of the Head is to create the ideal atmosphere and environment for learning to be promoted. He may want to look at the best use of the school day. If the argument is accepted that pupils and teachers work better in the morning then consider a six period morning with only two periods in the afternoon. Such an arrangement will also allow for a full supply of double periods when extended lessons are required. Finding the best calendar of term dates ideally maximising teaching days before examinations is another consideration.

The reasons why teachers do not deliver the goods are many and various. Some simply lack the necessary qualities and are unlikely ever to develop them. Teaching is a miserable career for those who can't cope and if you have such a member of staff he or she should be pointed in a different direction at the earliest opportunity. Others may have run out of steam in the classroom. A good deal of energy and enthusiasm is required to keep up with the rapid changes which have been occurring in both subject matter and teaching methodology. Someone who is not responding to these changes, particularly as the National Curriculum becomes a reality at Key Stages 3 and 4, is likely to be a liability.

A new Head is sometimes able to rekindle enthusiasm where past efforts may have failed. Some teachers will respond to a well planned programme of staff development (dealt with in a previous chapter); indeed all teachers should be expected to participate in such a programme – even the best need opportunities to develop their talents. Lively and interesting lectures and seminars on relevant topics are as useful in stimulating the staff as is a programme of speakers, visits and conferences for the pupils. There are general educational, pastoral and administrative functions which need to be fulfilled and some 'tired' teachers may be rejuvenated by a new challenge outside the classroom. With a reduced teaching load and an important new job, perhaps in charge of the timetable, examinations, the calendar or outdoor pursuits, many a flagging morale has been raised for the final part of a career.

Sadly there are sometimes nettles to be grasped. Someone who is not delivering in the classroom, and is unable or unwilling to take on other responsibilities and is exercising a dead-hand on colleagues, should be encouraged to take early retirement or to leave the profession. Such people spoil children's education and have no place in schools. Provided proper procedures are adhered to and a fair offer is made to the teacher, perhaps in consultation with the union, this process is not as difficult as some imagine.

The key person in improving academic standards is the Head of Department and there are few more important jobs for the Head than their selection. Assistant teachers should be developed for the role but it is chance if a department becomes available at just the right time for a rising star. Traditionally such appointments have had no time limits although there is a growing body of opinion that after

10 or 15 years most Heads of Department are ready for another job, if not another school. A similar view has been expressed about the appointment of Heads. A Head of Department who has run out of energy and enthusiasm is even more damaging than an assistant teacher. One famous Headmaster often greeted news of the departure of a member of his staff to another school with the comment "Good! Now I can get someone with a first class honours degree". A good teacher who has a first or a PhD may be a valuable asset but the emphasis must be on the 'good teacher' and for a Head of Department the ability to inspire and administer.

The role requires considerable ability and skills. First and foremost it requires academic leadership: a willingness to keep the department up-to-date with all the developments in the subject and its methodology. Apart from the considerable amount of reading involved, it requires regular meetings with HoDs from other schools, attendance at subject conferences and close liaison with, if not actual work for, examination boards and university entrance tutors. All these efforts will be ineffective if he lacks the organisational skills and the personality to put across what he has learned to his colleagues. Heads might well encourage HoDs and other teachers to belong to the relevant subject association, where much excellent curriculum development work is done. School membership is usually possible and desirable. The informal groupings within HMC – Rugby Group, Trinity Group, NW/NE Science Group *etc* – provide good opportunities for HoDs to exchange views on recent developments.

It was Shirley Williams when she was Secretary of State for Education, who decided that HMI would no longer carry out full inspections of independent schools. Visits from individual HMI continued and some schools called in teams or were visited within a sample. This process may be about to change again. The government has decided that private inspection teams shall visit maintained schools on a four or five year cycle. Independent schools are likely to come under pressure to set up similar arrangements. Currently HMC only inspects schools which are applying for admission or re-admission. The ISJC runs an inspection and advisory service and all applicants for membership and members of associations (other than HMC) on a ten year basis benefit from this accreditation service. Most Heads whose schools have been inspected find it a valuable, if expensive, experience. It provides them with an opportunity to discuss with independent and experienced practitioners weaknesses of which they are usually well aware. An ideal time for such an inspection is during the early years of a Headship, before the Head has become too involved in the level of performance or set in his ways. While inspection remains voluntary, new Heads might consider asking Governors to finance such an exercise. In a few years there may be no choice!

Much as one may learn as a Director of Studies or from regular meetings of the HoD committee it is the role of the Head to provide leadership in the academic life of the school. John Patten, in the White Paper *Choice and Diversity* (July 1992), says "Strong leadership ... means articulating a clear academic mission for the school, setting standards and creating a recognisable ethos ... they are necessary conditions for good management ... the better use of the school's resources and particularly harnessing the talents of staff to raise standards". No one under-estimates the magnitude of this task as thousands of pages of information and comment on academic matters cross the school's desk every year. HMC attempts to reduce the problem with briefing papers and summaries of important documents. Moreover it is impossible to be an expert in every field.

Everyone – teachers, parents, pupils – should be aware of the school's ethos and goals. Whether in the school's prospectus, speeches at prizegiving, sermons on Founder's Day, meetings with prospective parents, the message must come across clearly. Not all schools can emulate King Edward's Birmingham or Manchester Grammar or Winchester in achieving high academic standards. One of the strengths of the independent sector is that it can provide for all sorts and conditions of men. While it is right to strive for the best possible results which pupils can achieve it should not be at the expense of other important educational goals, not least the love of learning for its own sake and an awareness that the qualities which enable people to make a success of their lives go far beyond the academic.

There are few Heads who believe that the publication of league tables based on crude examination results does a great service to education. Academic results will depend to a large extent on the ability of the pupils entering the school. Those whose strong ambitions are to push their school up the league tables would do well to increase the number of applicants for entry and then to operate as selective an entry as possible, rigidly refusing to admit pupils of lower calibre even if it means the school becoming smaller. In times of recession this may not make economic sense. Nor would it necessarily produce a well-balanced community. What is essential is a programme of studies which suits the

Vivian Anthony, then Headmaster, escorts Prince Michael of Kent to inspect the Guard of Honour at Colfe's School.

needs and abilities of all pupils in the school and this principle will undoubtedly impose some limitations on who can be admitted. Schools which have an ethos akin to a comprehensive school and admit across the whole ability range will need a wide variety of courses if they are to do justice to all their pupils.

One of the criteria for membership of The Headmasters' Conference is that a certain proportion of pupils study and pass at least two subjects at A level. In 1991 only 22% of the age group achieved this goal and many young people were forced down this particular route for which they were not well-suited. HMC has expressed its support for a balance between depth of study traditionally associated with A level and breadth of education which for most people requires more than the study of just three subjects post-16. This conflict of goals is little nearer resolution now despite numerous initiatives. The government is on the one hand committed to A level as a means of preserving high standards and yet it sees the majority of young people following general courses with a strong vocational bias.

There are good reasons why Heads should be reviewing this post-16 curriculum particularly if they have a liberal admissions policy for their sixth form and quite rightly few are turning pupils away at present. Even able pupils would benefit from the inclusion of some vocational elements in their programme. There is much to be said for the use of modular-style courses in both A level and vocational areas. The use of BTEC modules in science, business studies or even European studies, performing arts, computing, caring or design, the excellent RSA courses in information technology or office administration, or the popular City & Guilds courses, to supplement A or AS level studies is to be commended.

The curriculum must be sufficiently flexible to allow able students the challenge of perhaps four A levels as well as their general studies programme. There is growing enthusiasm both from students and from higher education for a combination of arts and science subjects though this is certainly more demanding than narrow specialisation. There is much benefit to be gained from the continued study of a foreign language and some students prefer to do this with a vocational bias. Less able sixth formers may be better advised to take only one or two full A levels and to make up their programme with AS or modules from advanced or vocational courses. Although some schools make extensive use of AS level courses it cannot be said that they are universally popular. Moreover, two AS levels are significantly more demanding than one A level.

Apart from providing sixth forms with a broad, balanced and flexible curriculum it is just as important to maintain, establish or create a good working atmosphere. As part of an appraisal system Heads will visit classrooms and take an occasional stroll down the corridors, particularly when showing around visitors or prospective parents. Heads very soon become aware of the absence or existence of a good atmosphere.

Sixth formers have a significant amount of private study or, as they sometimes put it, 'free time'. It is an important but difficult job to persuade the students to use this time wisely. They must be encouraged to learn the relevant study skills. Moreover it is an essential part of their preparation for higher education. Success in this goal comes not only from the emphasis the Head puts on it but from real team work. All the teaching and boarding house staff, prefects and senior students have a role to play. A good library and reading room are invaluable. They must be places where students enjoy working. Well controlled and attractive common rooms not only provide opportunities for relaxation but they will remove from the library those who do not wish to work. The librarian's role is central. She needs not only all the skills of a librarian but the ability to preserve a working atmosphere. Most of all such an atmosphere comes from the ambition of the students. If they have a strong sense of wanting to do well, of competition, of pride in work well done and if they are constantly under challenge from teachers who set them demanding but reasonable assignments and if they have a good understanding of what they are trying to achieve, then a good working atmosphere should follow.

Too many schools suffer from the low expectations of their teachers. Students will do best when they are regularly pushed to the limits of their ability by inspired teachers. Judicious use must be made of praise and criticism. Opportunities for the latter may occur only too frequently and while the Head should not shrink from taking to task those who are wasting their opportunities it is important that he also sees those who are doing well. Prizes are not universally popular but it does allow the Head to praise not only the pupils but also their teachers and to build up confidence and expectations that others will follow the good example. This is the time to build pupils' ambitions, to persuade them to aim high, to strive for that Oxbridge goal.

The habits established in the lower and middle school will provide the basis for sixth form development. The introduction of the National Curriculum has changed some things but much will remain the same. It may offer new challenges which revivify the classroom teacher in the way the GCSE did for many, but it will not make a bad teacher good. Independent schools can decide whether or not to adopt the National Curriculum. In reality most academic schools already teach the NC subjects, though the need to fit other subjects – classics and the second language – into the curriculum means that technology and other creative subjects may not be given the same emphasis. When the only GCSE syllabuses available are those which conform with the NC, independence will not mean a great deal except in the matter of assessment.

Most academic schools have put great emphasis on regular testing and reporting as a means of keeping up standards. The July 1992 White Paper suggests that 'assessment and testing are the key to maintaining and raising standards'. Children generally respond well to testing and it gives them and their teachers an idea of what has or has not been learned. The doubts about NC testing arise partly from its sheer complexity and partly from its timing. Schools which admit pupils at 13 will not find it easy to prepare properly for KS 3 unless there is very close liaison with the feeder schools. The amount of time taken in teacher assessment and SATs, and the volume of recording and reporting required as well as quality assurance moderation, forces the Head to consider carefully what must be given up in order to do these things properly. Teachers' time is a scarce commodity. However it is not only inspectors and parents who can learn from the results of examinations and tests. A careful analysis carried out by the Head with the relevant staff will point up areas where performance can be improved or applauded. Some Boards supply reports on the performance of groups of pupils in an examination. It is right that Heads should take a close interest in teaching programmes, lesson preparation, homework set and the speed of marking.

There has been room only to concentrate on a few of the main determinants of academic standards and the way the Head influences them. More should have been said about involving parents, homework, reporting and particularly about Records of Achievement – well used they can be motivational and provide a means of rewarding those activities which do not lead to external exams. The staff ratio and set sizes, the danger of overloading willing teachers and persuading them that it is possible to overteach are other issues. The Government would have us consider rewarding teachers by performance, that is, children's performance.

Governors are expected to play a more important role in scrutinising a school's achievements. Indeed the 1992 White Paper says the objective is 'to put governing bodies and head teachers under the greater pressure of public accountability', but for independent schools there can be no greater pressure than that of the market. Schools which fail to raise their academic standards have but a bleak future ahead of them. By the evidence of examination results schools in The Headmasters' Conference have seen their academic standards rise significantly in the last decade. It will be a prime objective of all Heads to see that this process continues.

Chapter 12

Developing the Site

Geoffrey Parker
High Master, The Manchester Grammar School

Let us begin with a few plain and uncontroversial statements:

The style and even the nature of education is changing fast.

It will continue to change in the future, possibly at an even more rapid rate.

Competition between schools is likely to be with us for the foreseeable future, and in some areas may be fierce.

Teachers, especially those of real ability, will be more difficult to recruit.

Ambitious teaching programmes always cost money.

A government of any colour will always limit the amount of money allotted to schools.

Let us now clothe the bare bones with a little flesh. While much of what we seek as ultimate ends in our schools remains unaltered, the manner in which we carry out our daily tasks has changed, urged on in recent years by a government with a strong desire for changes and the political will to see them through. Teachers, ambitious to make best use of these initiatives and ready to introduce innovative methods into their teaching, have also made a significant contribution.

Fundamental reviews into almost all subjects have been carried out during the last decade and as a result they need different accommodation. More practical work in Science means more laboratories, fewer classrooms. In both English and Modern Languages more oral work has meant that the traditional classroom layout no longer suffices. Many subjects – History and Geography are good examples – are more 'resource based' and easy access to materials is essential if there is to be project work. Many departments would expect to use video material routinely as part of their teaching programmes. Drama too needs special facilities and some would deem a theatre to be not enough. The recent emphasis on creative studies – Art, Design and Technology – has meant the provision of expensive new or refurbished buildings and costly equipment.

Overlying all subjects is Information Technology, developing at what to the middle aged seems an alarming rate but exciting the young. In my own school, which installed its first mini-computer in 1978, we are now looking at our fifth generation of equipment. Within the next five years we expect to have IT in an appropriate form in all departments, and at the end of that period we know that we shall be rethinking our whole IT policy.

In sports and games more is expected by staff, pupils and parents. The same could be said of residential accommodation. Carpeted floors are relatively inexpensive to install and cheap to

Cricket at The Manchester Grammar School.

maintain, but separate accommodation for seniors, smaller dormitories for juniors, better Common Room provision, all cost money. It is hardly surprising that the sums spent in many independent schools during the last decade, either on new building or refurbishing old, are substantial and help to explain the steady rise in fees – well ahead of inflation during this period. That such enhanced facilities are appreciated by the staff who are privileged to enjoy them comes as no surprise. There is little doubt that prospective colleagues are attracted to a school with good facilities and are less enthused by premises that are run down and where there is little prospect of improvement. In the state sector there is a sharp contrast between those few schools which have been able to make improvements – CTCs are a good example – and the many who have not had the resources to cheer up tired buildings or, better still, replan existing accommodation to meet current and future needs. Frequently the consequence is low morale among the teaching staff.

The average tenure of a headship is ten years – occasionally a little longer – and during that time a Head should expect to spend on development sums estimated in millions. How many millions depends on the size of the school and the base from which development starts, but millions it will be and very few schools have easy access to that kind of money. Any newly-arrived Head will be looking at a development programme. Either one may already be in place or one may have to be devised. This and the raising of substantial funds will tax the Head's ingenuity and energy more than anything he or she does. Teaching and refereeing rugby will by contrast be pleasant relaxations, if there is time for either!

So how should a Head tackle this very serious business? Development programmes usually start with the Head, though occasionally they may come from elsewhere – a colleague, a Governor, perhaps a parent. Lest this may seem patronising, let me offer a word of explanation. Heads are brought in from outside to give a school fresh ideas, to see it with an outsider's eyes. Staff by contrast live with the place as it is and may be comfortable with developments with which they have been involved. More important, they are little concerned with planning and building regulations and usually ignorant of how a school is financed. Parents and Governors, as irregular visitors to the school, are unlikely to have either the professional insights or the intimate knowledge of the school's needs to offer anything other than general ideas.

Any Head will probably wish to conduct a comprehensive review of his school early in his term of office, will visit classrooms, laboratories and houses, listen to a wide range of opinions and will invite suggestions. This information will be listened to, rejected, synthesised. Even so, the Head's own contribution will be vital. Colleagues are either over-ambitious in what they demand or more frequently set their sights too low. The Head must decide the scale of development, balancing what the school needs against what is affordable over a particular period of time – reminding himself that he has a limited tenure and that much may have to be left to others. Building is heady stuff for the egotist!

A Head's dreams are not likely to become plans until he takes experts' advice – an architect to advise on the technical feasibility, the Bursar to offer advice on funding (though Bursars usually are either born or trained pessimists), a Governor (preferably the Chairman), to confirm that what is planned is something the governing body will support, senior colleagues who will advise on the acceptability of the project to the Common Room, and eventually the Common Room itself will wish to consider what is being proposed. Planning the order in which these individuals or groups are approached is a fascinating exercise in politics and will vary from school to school. However it is likely that the Head will talk, albeit informally, to the architect first because other people will be more impressed by learning of plans which have a reasonable chance of working, even though no doubt they will wish to modify the original ideas to the point where they become acceptable to all the major interest groups.

Indeed sharing ideas is a vital element in the success of any development project. This is partly because colleagues amplifying and improving the Head's own thoughts make it more likely that the project will be successful when it is completed and partly because the enthusiasm of others will be fired and their support gained so that the whole affair does not become the Head's flight of fancy. Detailed development, when the time comes, should be entrusted to others: a working party of the main users guided by the architect, the Bursar and a senior member of staff should be capable of seeing the work progress from outline drawings to the finished product. During this time the Head will be busy with other matters because the project has to be funded.

When it comes to raising the money, the Head should not be surprised to find himself very much on his own. Teaching colleagues will be indifferent, or even hostile, to fundraising. The Bursar manages money and does not raise it. Governors are too busy if they are young, working and active, or too old to be able to commit the energy that fundraising requires, though both groups may have valuable contacts to whom they can introduce the Head. A school is fortunate if its Governors are both influential and committed, and we should all be moving towards the time when Governors expect to be actively involved in this aspect of a school's life.

For these reasons, and because of the sheer scale of the operation, the Head needs professional advice and help. This may involve him in his first struggle. Few developments can be funded from surpluses, though they are valuable, and money for development as opposed to routine maintenance should certainly be included in every school's budget. 10% would be an excellent figure, 5% is what the Head can probably count on, but this will not be enough. Few schools have endowments, bequests are hardly a reliable way of raising money, and the events beloved of parents' associations raise useful but comparatively small sums. Involving the parent body in this way is valuable in getting them to take part in the 'improvements' to the school, but the most reliable way of raising money is simply to ask people for it.

"The average tenure of a headship is ten years - occasionally a little longer - and during that time a Head should expect to spend on development sums estimated in millions".

To do this the Head needs the help of an appeal director. Appeal companies and appeal directors are usually not liked – at least by some people. In the three appeals in which I have been involved I have regularly found objectors among Governors, colleagues, parents and former pupils. These are prejudices to be overcome because the support of the governing body is vital as they after all will be the employers of the appeal director. Although good appeal directors are not easy to find and are expensive, one must be found as he or she is central to the success of the whole operation. Amateurs – the well disposed retired Old Boy or Old Girl or former member of the teaching staff – are no longer good enough.

Professionals may work freelance or be employed by a company. In both choosing and managing the work of the appeal director, one must take great care and if necessary be quite ruthless. An appeal director who does not get on with a Head, or who does not create a good impression and inspire confidence, both inside and outside the school, has to go. This kind of ethic is alien to those of us who have spent our lives in the teaching profession and may be very disagreeable. Governors are frequently less squeamish and this reinforces the need to have the support of the governing body.

What should the appeal director be expected to do? First, he should explore the feasibility of raising the sum required. He would expect to interview prominent previous donors (if any), some Governors, representatives of the teaching staff, parents and former pupils. He should also see a selection of prominent prospective donors who have no known connection with the school – for example representatives of major companies and affluent individuals who are located within its catchment area. There is an element of luck in any prospecting of this kind, but making luck happen is an important aspect of any appeal. The director will discover whether they think the project advisable, whether they would support it financially and to what extent.

The amounts quoted during these interviews are a useful gauge of the feasibility of the appeal but should not necessarily be taken as being a final amount that the donor will give. Frequently donors can be persuaded to give rather more! He should ask them whether they would be prepared to help in other ways – serve on the committee, act as hosts at a meeting, approach other donors. During the research phase no money will be raised, yet the appeal director will draw his salary and pay his secretary. The expenses for telephone, fax, photocopier and travel must be found. Everyone in school will ask what he is doing and clearly this phase needs proper explanation, both formal and informal, to all interested parties so that confidence is sustained. Remember how suspicious everyone is!

The appeal director must also provide a plan of campaign. This involves the best order in which to approach donors, starting with those major givers whose large gifts help to make the whole enterprise credible and also making sure that the whole constituency is approached. Working out a timetable to make the best use of his and the Head's time is a lengthy and detailed task. The appeal director should advise the Head on the composition of committees, though the Head or Chairman of Governors will no doubt wish to approach individuals. The identification of a 'Campaign Chairman' is a crucial task.

The director should also service the committees, arrange times for meetings, produce papers and, in co-operation with the Head and Campaign Chairman, guide policy decisions. He should be responsible together with the Head and the relevant committee for producing any appeal literature and, when the appeal becomes active, arrange meetings and any entertainment and advise whoever is to lead the approach on the best arguments to deploy at that meeting. It is highly likely that the Head will lead and will himself ask the donor to 'consider' a specific sum. To the Head who finds this embarrassing I would say that it becomes easier the more frequently he does it, and the people you are dealing with will rarely feel affronted or embarrassed themselves. The world beyond school is used to doing business in this way and you will undoubtedly enjoy the glow of success when it comes.

Each approach, especially to major givers, needs careful thought and thorough preparation. It is worth noting that a director who works for a large and reputable firm frequently has access to information denied to the loner. Each group also needs a different approach. Charitable trusts usually like to see signs of 'self-help' from within the school community. Both colleagues and parents should be handled with a degree of sensitivity, though frequently they are among the most generous of givers. Former pupils generally do not have this reputation, though there are many notable exceptions. American experience suggests that alumni are a fertile source of giving – an idea which universities here in Britain are now beginning to develop and which should have a place in our schools. Building a database of former pupils, seeing them regularly at gatherings or individually, writing to them about the school's progress – all contribute to the building up of goodwill and a sense of being involved with the school. But it is a long-term process which may not yield immediate results.

Making friends and keeping them is an important function of an appeal, and it is worth considering how best this can be done. Major donors might be styled 'patrons', 'friends' or even 'second founders'. All who give should be recognised in some way – by plaques, dedication opportunities, by being invited to an opening or regularly and routinely to school functions. They should all be kept informed about the development and the fundraising. They need to know the progress of the project in which they should see themselves as investors. Clearly the Head cannot cope with such a workload by himself; the appeal director must help here too.

He must also help the Head to raise everyone's sights. The figures quoted earlier in this chapter stagger the older generation. Even if inflation is held within reasonable bounds, costs will surely continue to rise. The one-time gift of £100 may have seemed adequate once. For an affluent parent or former pupil, £1,000 per annum covenanted over five years (and five years is a good timespan for a development project) could yield nearly £6,700. "Stretching the giving over a period of years makes the larger gift more affordable" is a phrase that can be used to greater and lesser donors alike, and the appeal director will advise each individual on how he or she might give most effectively.

All this is a far cry from the 1960s when many independent schools first started seriously to appeal for funds. Much has changed during the last decade – Gift Aid and the reduction of covenants from seven to four years are two examples of changes in the law. But there is also far more emphasis on private giving and, regrettably for us, far more pressure on traditional donors. To that extent we operate in a tighter market and these trends may develop further. Changes to charity law may give all schools charitable status, and we are all likely to be more dependent on private funding if we are to keep our schools accessible. Nothing has been said in this chapter about bursary funding and the building up of endowments but clearly, if our costs continue to rise, our clientele will shrink unless we can reduce the fees to an affordable level. As the search for more funds becomes not only more intense but something we will think of as a perpetual need, the value of a permanent 'wealth creator' in the school, a business manager or development manager, becomes more obvious. The role is to sustain the momentum generated by the appeal at its most active phase, because only in that way will the school continue to raise money and retain its competitive edge. He will therefore find plenty to do and become as vital to the school's well-being as the Bursar who manages the money which the 'wealth creator' has raised. We have just appointed our first.

Chapter 13

The Boarding School Head

Richard Rhodes

Headmaster, Rossall School

The inclusion of a separate chapter on the Boarding School Head suggests that the role of the Head in a boarding school is different from his day school counterpart's and that it is an enlarged experience, in which additional skills and aptitudes are essential if the role is to be successfully executed. This is certainly the case.

Of course the essential ingredients for a 'good' school remain unchanged. The Head of a boarding school can expect to have similar demands made on him – professional development, academic skills and interests, management talents, overall interest in the pupils, discipline – as in any day school. There are however a number of particular areas where demands may be greater.

The Head of a boarding school can expect to be a combination of Lord of the Manor, parish priest, village 'bobby', social worker and odd job man to a degree unknown in a day school. This stems of course from the fact that he presides over a community which consists not only of pupils and academic staff. The resident ancillary staff and families of colleagues will make demands on a Head's time just as much as the pupils and staff.

Initially this community may well 'pull up the drawbridge' when the new Head arrives. Decisions on the use of buildings and maintenance schedules will be as important to the Housemaster's wife, whose redecorating expectations have been disappointed, as they will to the Head of Physics, whose new laboratory is not quite finished. How do you persuade an ex-Housemaster that his daughter, who has now left the school and is employed locally but still lives in the school, cannot have priority over pupils in the queue to see the school medical officer in the morning? Expect tensions when the schedule for refurbishing staff houses is published! When your wife is asked round to coffee, she can expect to hear all about this as well.

The community is always with you. This is of course a strength and a great source of challenge and joy. Your involvement with young colleagues – some of whom will marry and have young children in their time with you – provide that extra dimension to the normal professional function of the Head. They need looking after. Take an interest in their families, whether they have just been born or have recently graduated and are looking for a job. Aged parents of colleagues, whom you have come to know at the Christmas gatherings, will die and your concern and interest at these times will be well rewarded. Increasingly it seems the domestic tensions of modern marriages will be brought to your attention. These crises do not respect the clock.

It is arguable that the Head of a boarding school has to be more reliant on colleagues than might otherwise be. This is particularly the case with Housemasters and Housemistresses. The ability to appoint such people is essential to the success and smooth running of the school. The pressures on them are immense. They live surrounded by noisy, inconsiderate adolescents for 24 hours a day and they need to know they have your interest and support. Do not assume if you hear nothing from them means that all is well. It could mean that they don't want you to know how bad things are! It follows also that the skills of the Head in orchestrating discussion at Housemasters' meetings, in order to achieve a consensus or to reach agreement, will be fully tested. Housemasters and Housemistresses guard their charges very jealously! The Head should make endless excuses for popping into boarding houses on the most unexpected occasions.

Housemasters can also be immensely powerful and influential in a school. You are a mere new boy; they on the other hand have come up the hard way. You are a whizz kid who is quite likely to move on, while they slave loyally away until retirement. Why should they try anything new? After all, your successor will only want to change it again. More than one Head has bitten

Richard Rhodes: "The Head of a boarding school can expect to be a combination of Lord of the Manor, parish priest, village 'bobby', social worker and odd job man to a degree unknown in a day school".

the dust by failing to enlist the loyalty, support and co-operation of Housemasters. On the other hand they have no right to assume that they, rather than you, run the school. The sensible conduct of meetings and genuine processes of consultation are absolutely vital.

By its very nature the boarding school tends to stand against many of the social trends which bombard the adolescent. This is a very difficult area which is special to the boarding school Head in its relevance and intensity. There is a conflict too, much of the time, in that parents expect you to discipline their children and to stand against the 'disco' mentality and the standards which they invariably set at home. It will not be unknown for your disciplinary stance to be interpreted by a pupil as an example of unhappiness. With parents having told their child that if he is ever unhappy at school he can always come home, your firm discipline is easily undermined. Is the threat to expel a boy for having a pint of beer worth the loss of fees this year, let alone next year or the year after?

Your projection and promotion of the school is increasingly important nowadays when boarding is ceasing to be 'fashionable'. Your strategy needs to be clearly defined and well thought out. Schools' needs vary enormously. Some schools are well connected with good 'feeder' preparatory schools – others less so. A tactic for one school will not necessarily suit another. Nevertheless as a boarding school Head you must expect to see the vast majority of your parents personally. The Open Evening of a day school is not sufficient. You are after all going to oversee the most precious asset of any family – its children. The parents want to know if they can trust you. Modern thinking suggests that the Head sets the tone and the standards. You as an individual will be seen as the spearhead of your school's public relations and marketing. Never forget however that your best propaganda agents are your present parents. A positive comment will run right through a preparatory school or an ex-pat community overseas. Look after these people. They can make or break you! Keep your parents well informed about what is going on. They much prefer to hear from you than from a neighbour who has read about your school in the papers.

You will also have a role in the locality, despite the fact that the immediate community may send you few local children. Your school will have a name and reputation. Deal quickly and personally with any complaints. Neighbours, shopkeepers, police and bus drivers all need to be able to speak well of the school and its pupils. If there is a problem which is dealt with quickly and effectively they are more likely to remember that than the problem itself. Warn them if a helicopter is due to arrive and invite them to your plays and concerts. It is likely also that if you are the Head of a traditional and nationally renowned school, you will receive plenty of attention from the media. Whereas the day school is the focus of interest for the local newspaper, as boarding Head you are likely to receive calls from the other end of the land if someone has hit the limelight at home. It also seems that the higher your fees the more you are of interest to journalists.

It is then the totality of the experience in a boarding environment which makes all the difference. Whilst this explains in large measure the attraction of the job, it clearly can take its toll on the Head and his family. This is exacerbated by the inevitability that the boarding school of national renown is likely to have Governors who are a long way from the school and who perhaps appear only for the termly meeting. There are real dangers that the Head can become increasingly isolated, immersed in the pressures of paperwork, seemingly endless meetings and short of confidants. Add to this that the day is long and weekends tend to be busier than the week and the stamina so essential for this role is quickly eroded. When difficulties arise it is not always easy to find someone with whom to share them. Forcing an optimistic pace can take its toll and your every move is watched. Each word can be pondered over late into the night in the Common Room bar.

If the boarding Head cannot organise himself he will increase the stress and tension on himself and his family. His diary needs to be thoroughly planned. Regular meetings, teaching schedules, weekend commitments and absences must be clearly in place. Three diaries are needed – one for himself, one for his wife and one for his secretary. Keeping all three synchronised is a nightmare which has to be accommodated. He must ensure that plenty of time is earmarked for himself and his family. Make the best use of visits to other schools or meetings in other parts of the country. Take a night away and take your wife with you. If recruitment overseas is planned, persuade your Chairman that all your wife's (unpaid) hospitality to school guests could be recognised somewhat if she goes along too! Avoid the temptation to believe that you are indispensable. Quickly accept that your colleagues will think you are always away whatever you say and do.

In a boarding school it is much more likely that your home will be seen as the centre of hospitality than in a day school. It is perhaps a hard fact of life that you and your family will be required to extend endless hospitality to your Governors, colleagues, guests and visitors, as well as pupils. If the Head and his wife do not like doing this – and if you cannot train your children to smile and be polite, even if they are bored stiff – then the life of a boarding Head is not for you. The system in the school must be sufficiently efficient to enable you to function. Make sure that the Bursar and catering officer are aware of your expectations and requirements from the outset. There is no reason why your wife should slave over the cooker in order to give lunch to the bishop on Confirmation Day. The presence of visiting speakers, preachers and other guests will give you the chance to entertain colleagues at the same time. The boarding Head (and probably the day Head as well!) should not necessarily expect to have hospitality reciprocated. Your colleagues may not feel it necessary and many of your parents will assume it is all part of your function for which they have paid. Occasionally you will enjoy very generous and spectacular hospitality.

On the assumption that your boarding school has a greater range of buildings than the equivalent sized day school, you have to work well with the Bursar. He is likely to be in regular contact with your governing body who control the financial affairs of the school. Learn to work with him. Make

Rossall School: "The real challenge for a boarding Head lies in the ability to persuade colleagues that the weekends are part of the educational provision of the school".

sure that you are briefed about everything. Try to ensure that care of the plant is adequately covered. If this is not done then it will lead to tensions. Peeling paint will be seen as a school in financial difficulties. Dirty houses will not impress parents contemplating large fees. Inadequate food is always a source of discontent. Whilst these are present in every school, they are ever present and unavoidable in the boarding school.

On a day-to-day basis you will have more time and more opportunity to 'walk the job'. A visit to school breakfast or tea, in particular, will help you test the atmosphere of the school as well as being seen to check the quality of the food. Excuses can be made – a report on sports results for example – for boys and girls to visit you at home. This is the time to find out what is really going on. The extension of hospitality to pupils is a very conspicuous area where the boarding school has the advantage over the day school. It is also greatly appreciated and very enjoyable. From the parents' point of view, anything we can do to expand the social graces and experience of their offspring is warmly welcomed.

Reference was made earlier to the difficulties posed for the boarding Head by the social pressures outside school. In recent months many of our schools have received extensive press publicity as a result of disciplinary measures emanating from relatively 'unusual' incidents. Nevertheless the ability to reveal 'scandal' or 'sensational' behaviour is the stuff of which the tabloid press is made. By the very nature of the boarding school these activities, when they occur, will do so under your authority. Do not forget that they are going on everywhere and the day school Head can be glad that his children go home in the evening and at weekends. This will help you to keep a sense of proportion. Do not be tempted to sweep the issues under the carpet in the hope of avoiding bad publicity. If you fail to act on receipt of information and it is subsequently revealed that you did nothing, you will then be held equally culpable. You can rest assured that, if there is a problem, some of your children will reveal all to their parents. No credit marks will be awarded for inactivity on your part. By contrast, swift effective action, irrespective of media response, can be used by you to demonstrate your determination to enforce discipline and order.

These crises will tend to occur at weekends. Once the school adopts a less formal and more relaxed atmosphere – and there are no lessons or activities – then trouble invariably looms. The real challenge for a boarding Head lies in the ability to persuade colleagues that the weekends are part of the educational provision of the school. There is a responsibility placed on them to provide as much activity as possible. This is not easy with wives and families feeling a little neglected and colleagues tired and exhausted by the usual demands of teaching effectively in the classroom. This is the essential challenge of boarding. It has to be seen to be different from a day school education and it has to be seen to be worth the extra cost.

Another perhaps less tangible but nevertheless very important difference in a boarding school is the probability that there is a school chapel and that you have a Chaplain. A good Chaplain is invaluable. Try to see him as the parish priest for both staff and pupils. He is of course your appointment but you should be bold enough to give him a free rein. Respect the confidences which he holds and allow him free access to everything. Bring him to Housemasters' meetings, even if he doesn't wish to say anything. Many a potential difficulty can evaporate with the effective involvement of a good Chaplain. This is equally true for your Common Room as it is for your students.

The boarding school also has many other people whom you need to look after but who will also have an ear close to the ground. Matron, sister in the sanatorium, catering officer, groundsman, clerk of works and perhaps a secretary can all be used by the pupils as shoulders to cry on. They also know where the piles of cigarette ends are accumulating or where excess damage indicates persistent indiscipline. Gossip gleaned in the surgery queue or in the needleroom might help to avert a crisis. Always let it be known that you appreciate comments 'off the record' and unattributed. If the community senses that the Head knows what is going on, life will be much simpler.

Old boys and former pupils are an important part of the life of the school. Boarding schools can see their potential in their support on an international scale but also as prospective parents, irrespective of where they live. The Old Boys' Dinner circuit can be tedious unless you set out to enjoy it. Your presence is appreciated. The news you can convey helps in your projection of the school and you cannot expect them to rally to your support if you do not put yourself out. On the other hand remember that their image of the school froze on the day they left. Avoid public confrontation if the President of the Old Boys stands up and criticises you for taking girls. Of course, when he was at school it was a great school but now you have taken girls! Remember that the President is probably in business and if he failed to change things from time to time his business would not survive. Do not storm out or shout, even if the situation demands it and you feel that way inclined.

Can anyone possibly survive life as Head of a boarding school? The answer is clearly Yes. However consultation, delegation, relaxation are all essential if you wish to survive. You will need a sense of humour, an understanding that this is a way of life and not a job, a most sympathetic and understanding wife and family and good health. You will never be bored. You will never have a clear desk and you will never be able to misbehave in public.

That reminds me, I must take my wife out to lunch!

Chapter 14

The Management of Change

Michael Mavor
Head Master, Rugby School

Why change anything? The late Frank Fisher, Master of Wellington College, used to say "Stick where you are because other people will eventually catch up with you". Machiavelli, however, advises The Prince to make all the changes that matter in the first hundred days.

Whatever a new Head thinks and does, some change will be in the air from the first step: the glances and the gaze will be different, as will the walk, the asides, the tone, the strengths, the weaknesses, the doubts and the affirmations. Listen to the great Stoic philosopher Marcus Aurelius, Emperor of Rome and a constant solace to Wardens, Principals and Heads in their moments of anguish:

> "We shrink from change; yet is there anything which can come into being without it? What does nature hold dearer or more proper to herself? Could you have a hot bath unless the firewood underwent some change? Is it possible for any useful thing to be achieved without change? Do you not see then that change in yourself is of the same order, and no less necessary?"

That last sentence is the stunningly logical one. Before setting out to reform a school, one must instinctively and systematically (the two processes are separate) latch on to what is good; such things may be new to one in their cast and emphasis and will involve change in oneself. After that change in oneself change elsewhere is likely to be a positive process.

From deep roots and firm foundations one grows and develops. Tradition, the past, what is known and familiar are valuable in so far as they give a sure foothold, a place in this troublous life and confidence to share some certitude with others. Things must then move on. Those who are sceptical about change can perhaps take heart from the Christian foundation of many schools and from the fact that Christ, the turner of tables and the asker of many questions, said this: "Think not that I am come to destroy the law or the prophets; I am come not to destroy but to fulfil".

So before one makes any change one must be absolutely clear about the past and one's touchstones. Running a school is like producing a play: the text is already there and has been interpreted many times. You must shape it and cut it while remaining true to it and then choose your cast with infinite care though you will inherit some, like Bottom, who will want to play every part and who thrust themselves upon you. Where is your starting point? As a young assistant master in a staff play I once had to kiss the Headmaster's wife on stage. We were both hesitant. "It's simple", the producer said, "get your feet in the right position".

What kind of school do you want to run? What would you say now, not in the opening paragraph of your prospectus but to your wife or husband, in your heart of hearts, with a quiet whisper of truth? For you cannot be a good Head and you cannot manage change without such a knowledge. A fine school is not just there to teach Maths and English, to give the feel of oil paint across a rough canvas, to sing, to run, to have fun and to worship. Teilhard de Chardin once said that real happiness must involve not only the parts of our own existence, but an involvement in something greater than ourselves. What is it in your school that is greater than the parts so well described and illustrated in your prospectus? The stars in your sky may well be different from those in mine but it is by such fixed stars that all changes of course must be made so that the journey is one of fulfilment.

What actually happens in your school? Some of your early changes will involve routine. Routine is important; or if it isn't why on earth do we subject our pupils to so much of it? But it mustn't get in the way of what really matters: laser-like thought on every issue, listening to people, and being present at little things. So we must hone our routines to be as efficient as possible and to take as little time as possible; the preceding chapters in this book focus on this, but it may be worth mentioning a few things.

Get your secretary or administrative assistant to deal with as much outside mail as possible. Deal with internal mail first – one must never keep colleagues waiting. Use a portable dictating machine, put in the punctuation and insist on absolute accuracy. I am afraid there is a right way to spell yes and no! How well are inquiries and visits handled? Is every detail as welcoming and informative as you can possibly manage? Telephone one of your friend's schools and get him to telephone yours. Do you offer coffee or a meal? Is there a bathroom readily available? Do you have toys for younger children? What is the state of your home and office in terms of curtains, decoration and carpets? Are tours of the right length and done by the right people? At secondary level, for example, I am sure that the guide should be a pupil. What follow-up is there when people have registered? Do you send prospective parents newsletters, occasional invitations to concerts and plays, or the school magazine?

Do all of the arrangements for entry examinations and scholarships run smoothly? What positive and friendly links do you have with local or national newspapers, radio and television? Who makes all the arrangements for governors' meetings and are these as good as they might be? How often do they have drinks with colleagues or pupils? Do you have regular weekly meetings with your Bursar, Deputy Head, Director of Studies, Chaplain – whoever? How often do you see your Chairman and how often do you send bits of positive information to other Governors – or telephone them? Is ample time given for Heads of Department, Housemasters, prefects or whoever to contribute to the agenda of meetings, and are full and accurate minutes circulated within two days of the meeting? How carefully do you go through your diary with your wife or husband a term and a year ahead and how realistic have you been in what you are undertaking? Do you combine events so that when you are in London you can visit a son or daughter, a department store and a feeder school? Are you giving enough time for various appointments and are you punctual with them? When and in what situations do you see your pupils?

It is no bad thing to plan dinner parties or more casual entertaining a term in advance, just as it is helpful to know who is likely to be staying with you and to keep the first hour on Monday morning free to deal with the odd wild boar and to go over the week with your secretary. The routines for emergencies – fire, flood, a bomb scare, press hounds and major health scares – all need to be clear to everyone. For the big visits a certain pattern of thought and planning has to be developed and it is worth spending a day with a good army adjutant. Whatever the ultimate purpose of the armed services, they do know how to operate systems and how to operate them when half of the troops are dead – in our more civilised surroundings it's when they and we are half-dead – when communications are bad, when they are under heavy attack and when the jocks are questioning the absolute wisdom of the last order.

Change is closely linked to routine, particularly in the lives of boys and girls, and is therefore always to do with practical matters. "We must act our dreams with open eyes to make them possible" Lawrence of Arabia once said. Change

Rugby School: Two younger pupils meet the Head Master, Michael Mavor, in the Upper Bench. The stained glass windows portray previous Head Masters stretching back to the sixteenth century.

therefore requires planning, methodical persistence and careful timing. Here is Marcus Aurelius again:

"If you were asked to spell the name Antoninus, would you rap out each letter at the top of your voice, and then, if your hearers grew angry, grow angry yourself in turn? Rather, would you not proceed to enunciate the several letters quietly one by one? Well, then: remember that here in life every piece of duty is likewise made up of its separate items. Pay careful attention to each of these, without fuss and without returning temper for temper, and so ensure the methodical completion of your appointed task."

The two most important things that a Head has to do, in practical terms, are the appointment of good staff and the recruitment of good pupils. Nothing else matters as much. With the right people in the right place at the right time on the staff, and committed, decent honest boys and girls coming into the school, change will be much easier. It is therefore worth reviewing all of your routines for interviewing and selecting staff and pupils.

It can be most helpful to ask colleagues to write to you on one sheet of paper with their observations on what needs to be preserved and nourished in the school and on what improvements they would like to see and how they would put these into effect. One learns a lot about the school and about the staff. . . .

It is important to know where the oomph really lies in a school, to talk with slightly disillusioned middle management and to be aware of the hierarchies. When I arrived at Rugby from Scotland I was slightly puzzled by some of the bowing of heads that seemed to go on in the first Chapel Service. I asked the School Marshal, an ex-Regimental Sergeant Major, to explain things to me: "Well sir, you can bow to the altar if you want, sir. You can even bow to God if you like, sir. But your predecessor, sir, he always bowed to me, sir".

Open meetings with parents are useful ways both of gathering information and of imparting it. Once one has been in a school for a while a questionnaire can be useful. I have open meetings too in boarding houses, at which boys and girls can ask me questions and give me their views. I find that prefects' meetings work best with an agenda and accurate minutes. A reasonably formal system of appraisal or staff development is essential: all sorts of good ideas spring from this and it is almost always a thoroughly positive process. Colleagues need to be reassured and taken along with one; I don't hesitate now to discuss even quite big issues in an experimental way with any member of staff. This is a sort of touchline tap dancing. Many a good idea has come to me from a colleague under a tree on the boundary or in the hall of a department.

Even more important are the subcommittees which investigate the possibilities for change, either on a regular basis or with a particular brief. These have to be encouraged and monitored. I have found it very helpful to have a central committee, consisting of the Second Master, Director of Studies, Director of Activities, Chaplain, Bursar and two colleagues who change every year; this meets each month and does its best to think big and to bounce ideas around.

Most change or involvement requires money and there needs to be a positive, creative tension between the Head and the Bursar that enables things to happen. Non-teaching staff are important. They often have shrewd observations to make and certainly deserve to be told face-to-face of the implications of any changes that are to be made; these are sometimes very considerable for them.

The really big changes must be discussed in detail with the Chairman of Governors. Good Chairmen will welcome regular telephone calls that present them not with problems but with good news and a selection of observations about the school. Such communication provides a sound foundation for discussion of a profound issue. The same applies to a lesser extent to all Governors! It is important to keep in touch, perhaps at random, with all of them so that your recommendations for change are not being put to strangers. I suspect that many of us communicate too little with our Governors.

I prefer to discuss possibilities for change with smaller groups of pupils (a year group would be the largest) rather than floating ideas in a whole-school assembly. Old Boys and Girls? Talk to them, listen to them, write to them – and get on with the changes you have decided to make. What are the facts? What are the issues? What do I have to do? Who do I have to tell? Even small changes have to be communicated, sometimes several times, to all those affected by them. Big changes may demand very carefully timed mass mailings to parents, Governors who were absent, former pupils (several different categories of letter may be needed), prep, primary or secondary school heads – and a word to one's wife or husband!

If after reading these chapters you feel daunted, don't worry. I was once rushing to catch a night sleeper from Euston Station. I though it was an open platform, was running late, and rushed towards the train. "Hey, man," came a cry, "Where do you tink you are goin?" I turned round abashed to see a huge black lady waving her ticket-puncher at me. I went back and as she clipped my ticket she asked me what I did for a living. I told her and then said that I was sorry, I had thought it was an open platform. She gave me my ticket, smiled hugely and said, "Don't worry, Headman, you can't know everytink".

Chapter 15

And finally . . . the School's Philosophy

The Rev Dominic Milroy, OSB
formerly Headmaster, Ampleforth College

One of the most revealing recent developments in the educational world has been that of the school prospectus. This is not just a result of market forces, although it is now commonly accepted that good marketing has become an essential part of good management. My own school, like many others, survived happily for years without a prospectus: all there was to offer prospective parents was a single sheet of grey paper giving the essential data as cryptically as possible. It was only when parents started commenting that this system was "designed to repel" that we were obliged to become more self-aware and more explicit in defining and illustrating the central aims and objectives of the school.

For this is what a good prospectus now does. It represents not only a marketing tool but a mission statement. The preparation of a mission statement is an exacting task. It requires accuracy, honesty, comprehensiveness and imaginative vision. It is more than a description of what the school is; it is a philosophical statement about what the school is intended to be. This requires a clear understanding not only of the original purposes of the foundation but of the many ways in which those purposes have been developed or enriched by history and by circumstance. It also requires a clear perception of the balance between aims which are easy to quantify (for example high academic standards, range of acitivities) and those which are by definition unquantifiable (for example the incalculation of honesty or of a strong sense of community). Such a perception is hard to translate into a strong and convincing statement: descriptions or activities which are common to all schools can easily become repetitive and banal, and excursions into the unquantifiable (for example 'the school prides itself on being a caring and happy community') can trivialise important themes unless their real meaning is spelled out with subtlety and care.

The concept of a mission statement implies of course that there is a mission to state, *ie* that the school does have a philosophy or a purpose which both unites it with other schools and distinguishes it from them. It is to be expected that the philosophy of one good school will have a great deal in common with that of another. Indeed it is an extremely interesting fact that schools can discover so many different ways of expressing certain fundamental educational objectives which are in practice identical. It is equally true that schools vary, sometimes slightly, sometimes more profoundly, in the emphases which they place on particular educational goals. This tension, between sameness and variety, lies at the heart of all education. It is a particular feature of our national tradition, which has been characterised (in both maintained and independent sectors) both by a strong sense of conservatism and uniformity and by an eccentric leaning towards innovation and experiment.

It is fashionable at this particular moment in our history to fall in with the prevailing lament that our schools are not competing effectively with their opposite numbers in Germany or Japan. It is still arguable however that the 'models' offered by our national system are intensely interesting, both because of their variety and because of the confused but compelling national interest in the philosophy which underlies them all. In most modern cultures it is taken for granted that education is, quite simply, an agency of the state and that its 'philosophy' is co-extensive with that of the state. British education is uniquely and stubbornly resistant to this assumption. This may be in some respects a weakness, but it is likely to be a source of strength in the long term. This is because, in societies which are increasingly monolithic and centralised (and therefore ever more likely to impose uniform patterns of practice), our own attitudes towards education continue to generate the same tensions between variety and uniformity, between innovation and conservatism, which have always characterised it. It cannot be an accident that the government's recent White Paper is entitled *Choice and Diversity*. These tensions are still capable of eliciting a passionate response to questions related to the philosophy of education – questions which, in other cultures, are quite often not raised at all.

It is relatively easy to give 'philosophical' expression to a school's *special* features, *ie* those which distinguish it objectively from other schools. These may be closely related to the raison d'être or identity of a particular school, as would obviously be the case for many religious foundations, as well as for schools concentrating on meeting a particular need; or they may be more circumstantial, arising out of a school's location or chosen preference, in which case it is less a question of identity than of emphasis. There must be very few schools indeed which would not claim to be 'special' in any way.

Most of the distinctions fall under one or more of the following general headings: the school's relation to, and service of, a *wider society*, its relation to the *phases* of education (primary, secondary *etc*), its tradition and policy with regard to *gender*, its level of *selectivity*, whether based on academic or on other criteria, and its identity in relation to particular religious, civic or cultural bodies (for instance some foundations are specifically denominational, others most specifically not so). There is room under these headings for a huge diversity of tradition, particularly as none of them necessarily implies a straight choice between radical alternatives but rather the possibility of a wide range of differing emphases.

A school's relation to the society outside it, to what is often called 'the wider community', may vary quite deeply both in principle and in emphasis. There can be no doubt here that the obvious 'norm' arises from a school's place in its own locality – its relation with a particular neighbourhood and with the families and sub-groups (parishes, districts *etc*) which constitute it. For the vast majority of schools, of whatever phase or sector, this factor is crucial. It does not however imply anything resembling uniformity of style. The relationship of a village primary school to its neighbourhood is profoundly different from that of a large urban comprehensive, a suburban preparatory school, a CTC or a selective grammar school. In each case the ties with the neighbourhood are perceived differently, largely because there are many ways of describing or defining what a 'neighbourhood'

Rev Dominic Milroy: "My own school, like many others, survived happily for years without a prospectus".

actually is. Nowadays a neighbour is not necessarily a next-door neighbour but may rather be linked by common interests of convenience, economics or need.

The concept of the local community is extremely complex and implies a network of overlapping and interpenetrating interests, not to mention a good deal of tension. There is no such thing as a single ideal educational system capable of serving all these interests and resolving all these tensions. Governments, local authorities, churches and independent foundations have, according to their given role, imposed or offered a wide range of schooling. In terms of community-building, every solution has had both its strengths and its weaknesses. Just as the old tradition of the selective civic grammar schools both served and divided the community, so also (in different ways) does the vast comprehensive, the 'consortium' or the CTC, for which the notion 'neighbourhood' may be so amorphous as to lose any real meaning. A local selective independent secondary school may both meet a real demand and create its own community of neighbours, but it may also in other respects diminish rather than enhance the sense of a united locality. The present emphasis on cost-cutting, marketing, competition and standardisation, together with the extension of grant-maintained status, may indeed raise 'standards' in many areas, and may effectively enhance parental choice, but there is no evidence of a corresponding enhancement of what is still perceived by many as one of the essential requisites of a good local school – a strong and positive relationship with its locality.

Two conclusions emerge from this complex and shifting pattern of competing philosophies. First there is not likely to be any universal 'model' that will establish itself, either in practical or in philosophical terms, as the desirable educational solution for all. The structures and needs of modern society are simply too complex and imply too many competing interests. Secondly it is up to individual schools, of whatever kind, to build their own philosophies of neighbourliness within the pragmatic constraints of their situation. As in other areas of a nation's life we are moving away from a time of centralised ideologies into a 'mixed' system in which public and private sectors collaborate, and in which long-term success will depend less on imposed solutions than on local initiatives.

It is to be hoped that it will remain possible to emphasise the need for collaboration rather than see it swamped by the prevailing cult for competition. In a deep sense the concept of competition (however acceptable it may be in general terms) is potentially damaging to the wider interests of schools as a whole. This is primarily because children, whatever their individual talents or social background, should never be regarded simply as products, like Weetabix or Jaguars. There are too many unquantifiable factors for education to be regarded *predominantly* in terms of productivity, and we shall always need teachers who are willing to devote themselves to the welfare of those whom the world regards as failures.

Fortunately there are many schools in both the maintained and independent sectors where this last point continues to be taken for granted, whatever the pressures of league tables and the success-ethic. Most of the schools which serve a neighbourhood (in whatever way) start from the assumption that their job is to serve a wide ability range and that their evident success-rate will be at best unpredictable. Independent schools have also become more imaginative and flexible in relating to their locality, and this is increasingly likely to include a collaboration with maintained schools which are having to learn how to handle their enhanced independence from local authorities with regard to budgets and policy.

The norm by which schools interpret their relationship with the wider community is rooted generally in a set of local relationships. This is not exclusively the case. There are schools, usually (but not invariably) independent, whose links are with a community which is nationally rather than locally based. In particular, most of the boarding schools are either religious foundations or were created to meet a particular demand. In modern terms our society consists of and caters for a pluralistic network of overlapping minorities, which are in some respects subsumed into a relatively homogenous culture and in other respects distinct from it. In the maintained sector this fact is reflected above all by the dual system. This system makes, as it were, a philosophical statement about the relationship between the secular state and its Christian roots, and it is not surprising that it has often been under threat. The latest threat comes from the presence of religious minorities which are not Christian and which are less fully absorbed into the national culture. In the long run the fate of the dual system may well depend on the resolution of these factors; either way the implications will be very great.

In the independent sector there remains a very strong tradition in favour of 'special' philosophies ranging from the denominational to the 'progressive' and including an emphasis either on particular fields of human achievement (such as music) or on an enhanced 'holistic' curriculum in which outdoor activities (including particular sports) play a large part. The 'philosophy' of these schools is of radical importance to discerning parents and may make available to their children a type of formation and a realisable excellence which are available nowhere else.

The pressure in modern society towards sameness and towards a certain levelling down of cultural aspirations gives added importance to the preservation of institutions which cultivate *difference*. This must constitute one of the greatest arguments in favour of a strong independent sector, committed to the cultivation of 'minority' philosophies, whether religious or other. It is no accident that the model of the British independent school is increasingly sought after in cultures which are either severely damaged by an imposed cultural sameness (Eastern Europe) or threatened by something similar (Japan).

The other headings under which the philosophy of a school may be distinctive, either deeply or as a matter of emphasis, may be more quickly dealt with – partly because some of them have already been touched on. Schools often acquire their identity and purpose because of their association with a particular *phase*. The 11-16 comprehensive, the 13-18 boarding school, the 8-13 preparatory school (often with its pre-prep phase), the sixth form college – each of these will rightly concentrate on the aims and objectives associated with the needs of their particular phase (or series of phases) and on the constraints and challenges which they face in the context of *transfer*, the passage of a pupil from one phase of schooling to another, or from schooling to adult independence. All phases of schooling are at one level self-contained whilst being at another a preparation for what follows.

Different kinds of school will develop this balance in different ways: their 'philosophy' will depend on their being aware of the tensions involved, as also on their perception of the interaction between academic needs on the one hand and personal and social ones on the other. Thus there is one cycle with a rhythm marked at 11, 14, 19, and another where the 'natural' breaks are seen to occur at eight and 13 and 16. The very concept of the 'staying-on rate' implies that schooling after 16 is perceived (by some) as an 'extra', whilst in many schools the presence of a taken-for-granted sixth form is pivotal. The implications for staffing are considerable. Each school will have, as part of its philosophy, a clear statement of how it responds to the needs of the phase in which it specialises. It will also be sensitive to possible shifts in the articulation of the phases in schools as a whole.

The fact that most schools are and usually have been co-educational makes the existence of single-sex schools (and the philosophy that goes with them) all the more interesting. There is in a way less need for a co-educational school to have a particular philosophy: it is after all only an echo of society as a whole, although the case of a boarding school may introduce other factors too obvious to need stating. The single-sex school clearly stands as a distinctive *alternative* to what happens naturally, and its philosophy will take up this challenge. The segregation of the sexes during infancy and youth has its exemplars in the animal kingdom and has many antecedents in the history of human culture. There is no space here to rehearse the arguments. Once again it is an observable fact that our national culture has proved to be adept at providing alternative models, each of which has its justification and its appeal, and the existence of which provides a healthy bulwark against excessive uniformity. In any case the long-term survival of single-sex schools is likely to be decided by the law of supply and demand.

Perhaps the most contentious of the areas of distinctions is that involving selection. A school which selects its pupils, whether on academic or on other grounds, is clearly wholly different from one which does not, and the existence of selective schools clearly affects the character of parallel non-selective ones. The philosophical questions which arise here are questions not so much about the purposes of education as about the nature of society as a whole – the tension between egalitarianism and choice. It is to be remembered that the word *élitism* has the same roots as the word *choice*, and it is difficult to envisage a situation in which one could exist without the other. The ideological clash between egalitarianism and élitism has had pretty murky history on both sides, and it could be argued (for reasons already given) that the future lies in a truly conscientious search for a balance between them in a society which aims to be both compassionate and free.

It is not easy to balance the rights of the many against the manifest needs of the few. It is worth pointing out that in academic terms this is what many independent schools have been trying to do for a long time and their experience of a 'mixed' system, partly selective, partly non-selective, provides a useful philosophical model for at least part of the solution. But the difficulty here is a real one and is compounded by that of fee-paying: it will not simply go away quietly. What is important at this stage is that the philosophy of the independent sector should be increasingly seen to be one which is contributing to the nation's educational provision rather than as militating against it. This means at least that we must all 'clear our minds of cant'.

The distinctiveness of denominational schools, or of those (like the great grammar schools) which are specifically civic or secular, is too obvious to need much comment. In an increasingly pluralist society however their purposes need spelling out, probably more so than in the past. The models represented by institutions which belong to distinctive religious and cultural minorities become more important as society as a whole becomes more monochrome. They not only provide focal points for the preservation of particular value-systems; they also represent, within the national system an alternative cultural and spiritual standpoint from which accepted contemporary attitudes may be seen in the perspective of a longer history.

Underlying the various types of distinctiveness which provide the cutting edge of a school's philosophy, there must always be an even clearer grasp of the purposes of education as a whole. One might have expected here to encounter a large measure of quiet agreement and not much need to be too explicit. This is however far from being the case. Insofar as there ever was a consensus on the purposes of education in British schools, it was based less on Plato, Rousseau or Newman than on a mixture of instincts rooted in countless examples of what nowadays would be called 'good practice'. It is perfectly clear from the recollections of many distinguished writers that these examples of good practice are often more than off-set by similar cases of bad practice, and that the so-called 'public schools' represented a less coherent set of educational values than those which increasingly characterised the village schools and the great urban grammar schools. The great public school reformers like Arnold and Thring were the exceptions rather than the rule, although their influence proved in the long run to be profound.

Profound, but vulnerable. Recent reforms have brought many changes both in structures and in attitudes. Most of these changes have been sociological rather than strictly educational, but the consequences for schools have been great – the dislodging of the classics, the dismantling of the grammar schools, the gradual acceptance of the rights of youth to have its own 'culture' within the school system, the tolerance extended to permissive styles of conduct, the adoption of utilitarian goals within the curriculum. Each of these changes has found vocal 'philosophical' support in many quarters and has met a certain amount of vociferous opposition. There has been, however, little in the way of the development of a strong and coherent philosophy of what schools must be in order to absorb and to 'civilise' these deep changes, *ie* to educate modern children (*as they are*) without losing their own identity as schools.

The most recent reforms of all have tended to suggest that industrialists and parents should be ultimate arbiters of how schools should be run. The implications of these suggestions are profound, particularly with regard to the integrity of the teaching profession as a specialisation in its own right, and with regard to the corresponding identity of the school as an institution with a specific role in society. The questions thus raised are of profound philosophical importance and, unless they are

"In most modern cultures it is taken for granted that education is, quite simply, an agency of the state and that its 'philosophy' is co-extensive with that of the state. British education is uniquely and stubbornly resistant to this assumption".

answered, we are in for a lot more muddle – a muddle which will deter many potential excellent teachers from joining the profession.

I would suggest that there are certain absolutely essential affirmations that schools (of whatever sector) must make if they are to retain their identity and to re-establish their own confidence and that of teachers. These affirmations might be summarised as follows.

First the role of the school is complementary to that of parents and of home but radically different from it. The school as a professional institution is responsible for ensuring that children encounter, and master to an appropriate degree of competence, what we now call their *entitlement*. In the technical terms of the National Curriculum, this entitlement covers an agreed range of subject content and of skills, but in terms of the school's professional role it goes much further than this. Children are entitled to acquire a developing 'ownership' of the culture to which they belong. This culture is on the one hand rooted in an accumulation of human experiences which belong to the past and on the other pointing towards a set of opportunities which belong to the future. Left to themselves children always tend to get trapped in the preoccupations and attitudes of a very limited present. Thus the school's curriculum, both in its general shape and as applying to the content of particular courses, is one of the central expressions of the school's philosophy. The formulation of this curriculum is part of the school's professional duty, and the 'delivery' of it belongs to the professional competence of teachers as much as the carrying-out of an operation belongs to that of a surgeon.

This point is worth stressing for two related reasons. In the first place there is a growing tendency to downgrade the professional integrity of teachers in favour of that of the state, of industrialists or of parents, *ie* to suggest that school is little more than an agency or tool of government, of business or of society as a whole. The second reason is related to this in that teachers have to some extent brought this downgrading upon themselves. Far too often the central entitlement of children has simply not been delivered. School-leavers who cannot read or count, and who have been allowed to conclude that Shakespeare is less 'relevant' than Jilly Cooper, have been betrayed. But the answer to this must still lie in the hands of the teaching profession in general and of schools in particular. Only the school is in principle sufficiently disinterested to ensure that the curricular entitlement of children is protected from distortions imposed from without.

The second major role of a school is to be a *community of transition*, one which will help children, both academically and pastorally, to negotiate the passage from childhood to adulthood. Here again the role of the school is complementary to that of parents. The language of the market-place may suggest that parents be viewed increasingly as customers or as clients, but no good school will go down this road. In accepting a child, the school engages in a process of collaborative parenthood, enhancing the influence of strong parents and compensating for that of those who for whatever reasons are more frail. Adolescence can be a long and complex experience, and perceptive parents will always acknowledge that the supportive community of a school and the expertise of particular teachers are of irreplaceable importance in helping individual children to emerge as adults in their own right, strong and discerning in their capacity to relate in a balanced way with their families, their peer group and other adults.

The third aim of the school is linked to the other two. It is to foster *habits of learning*. These are not acquired solely in the classroom, and they go well beyond the range or information and skills with which their academic or vocational courses will equip them. All children have by nature a capacity and a desire to learn, but the transformation of this into a habit is difficult. The delight of discovery must be followed through by persevering and patient study. True learning in whatever field demands sustained attention, fidelity to what has been learned previously, a developing scepticism about received opinion and a taste for complexity. It has as much to do with the pursuit of goodness as with that of knowledge and fosters discernment in personal relationships as well as in professional work or study. In this sense the deepest goal of education is growth in wisdom.

Fourthly a school has the opportunity to foster, by the way it 'shapes' its own life, a *sense of balance*. It is neither an academic factory nor a holiday-camp, but has a carefully constructed rhythm based on a hierarchy of priorities. An *holistic* overall curriculum is one in which all activities have their own value and in which care is taken to prevent any single area (*eg* exam success or sport) from receiving undue prominence. The emphasis will vary from school to school, but a good school will always be able to defend the particular balance for which it has opted. The search for balance implies a fairly complex value-statement and always lies at the heart of a good prospectus.

Children are entitled when they go to school to find themselves in a community which will introduce them to their own culture, support them in their journey towards adulthood, teach them habits of true learning and give them a balanced sense of values. At the end of the process they will of course have made their own judgements and decisions with varying degrees of wisdom. A business enterprise or a factory may be able to guarantee the success of the product but a school cannot. Fortunately human children are too varied, too mysterious, too unpredictable to be easily manipulated or classified.

Dr Arnold, in a sermon preached in Rugby Chapel in 1840, enumerated the six 'evils' with which schools have to contend – profligacy, falsehood, cruelty, disobedience, idleness and "a prevailing spirit of combination in evil". Those with any knowledge of children, of families or of schools will readily acknowledge that human nature does not change much, and that those who are professionally committed to the education of the young are doing an extremely difficult job. A school is a crucible in which young human beings are testing out their own instincts and unformed value-systems against those which adult society is trying, with varying degrees of enlightenment, to make accessible to them. It is possible that the future of human civilisation depends on the outcome. There can be few human activities so difficult, so frustrating and so rewarding. In the long run any society which does not (at every level) value its teachers and its schools will have to pay an unforeseen price.